£7,00

Riding for Gold

Riding for Gold

*50 Years of Horse Trials
in Great Britain*

Foreword by HRH The Princess Royal

Compiled and edited by Barbara Cooper
Text by Jane Pontifex

Designed and typeset by Hugh Johnson
Editorial Assistants Clare Harris and Lucy Grayson

Published in Great Britain in 1998 by
Compass Equestrian Limited
Cadborough Farm
Oldberrow, Henley-in-Arden
Warwickshire, B95 5NX

ISBN 1-900667-35-5

A catalogue record for this book is available
from the British Library

Colour origination by Reed Digital, Ipswich, Suffolk

Printed in Spain by Bookprint SL

Frontispiece Prince William's first official engagement
was in 1991, at Badminton: presenting the winner,
Rodney Powell with the trophy for the owner of the
most successful horse sired by an HIS stallion (The
Irishman).

Contents

Foreword

BUCKINGHAM PALACE

Having been involved with horse trials for the greater part of my life, particularly the late 1960s and '70s, I have read this picture history with great interest. It has brought back many happy memories of the people, the places, the sporting encounters, and the fun. It has also reminded me of the unsung services rendered - mostly voluntarily - by organisers and helpers over the years.

The decade-by-decade summaries, tracing the growth of the sport from its fairly haphazard beginnings to its present well-ordered structure, make absorbing reading. In 1952 there were some half-dozen trials; today there are over 160 - most of them one day events, which are the backbone of the sport. All of the longest-running, as well as some of the most picturesque, are shown on these picture-packed pages.

The title of the book is certainly very apt. No other sport in this country can compare with ours when it comes to a tally of international honours. Every gold medal that has ever been won by British teams and individual riders, from the 1956 Olympics to the 1998 European Pony Championships, is illustrated here.

I hope that this record of eventing's first fifty years will give pleasure to all who follow the sport, and that it will provide inspiration to the younger generation of riders.

Anne

Editor's Note and Introduction

The idea for this book came from Tim Taylor, who took the trouble to read the minutes of all the horse trials committee meetings, dating back to 1948. Finding them to be of more than passing interest, he keyed them into his word processor and printed them out. He also compiled a chronological chart of all the events that have ever taken place.

As the only other book on the subject, *The Horse Trials Story* by Lt-Colonel C.E.G. Hope, had been out of print for many years, Tim felt that it was time for a new one, and asked Jane Pontifex if she would collaborate with him in writing it. They then discussed the idea with us at Compass Equestrian, and we happily agreed to be the publishers.

Our original intention was to produce a textual history with illustrations, but for various reasons the illustrations took over, and we decided that a year-by-year picture history would be more appealing.

Thanks to the support of Arnold Garvey, Editor of *Horse and Hound*, we have had access to the best equestrian photographic library in the country. We have also had the invaluable help of organisers and competitors, who have provided unique items from their personal albums. The BHTA's collection of programmes filled in some notable gaps.

For local interest we have included *all* the horse trials in Tim Taylor's chart, even if they only occur once. They appear alongside the decade-by-decade summaries. The events featured – each in the year when it started – have been selected principally as a tribute to those who have given long and distinguished service. If there are any obvious omissions, they are not due to lack of effort on our part; in some cases, requests for co-operation went unheeded. We also found, to our dismay, that many photographs relating to the first two or three decades had been lost or destroyed, or that the photographers had disappeared from the eventing scene.

Interspersed with the pictures of national events are illustrations of our international gold medallists, team and individual, from Olympic Games to Pony Championships, all of them brought together in one book for the first time.

No sport has achieved so much for Great Britain and been given so little public recognition. It is considered by some newspaper and TV sports editors to be 'élitist', which may be why they give it such limited coverage. Yet, far from being élitist, it is a great leveller – as any spin doctor would know if he or she had ever been spun.   *B.C. 1998*

Introduction

Horse Trials is a rather inadequate name for an equestrian sport which challenges every quality, every talent, both physical and mental, that horse and rider can muster between them. The second day's speed and endurance is the most important test – satisfying, perhaps, some primitive urge to gallop away across the countryside, surmounting all obstacles, in order to arrive, undaunted, at the appointed destination – and every bold rider with a talented horse wants to prove it in competition.

The sport originated in Europe as a test of

the basic training and general competence of a cavalry charger, hence its original name, the Military. As a contest for the all-round horse and rider it demanded no great athleticism, power or turn of speed on the part of the horse, no particular expertise on the part of the rider – just the discipline of basic training, courage, stamina, a cool head, a partnership built on mutual trust and confidence.

After its introduction as an equestrian event to the modern Olympic Games of 1912, thanks to the vision of count Clarence von Rasen, the competition went through various permutations of the main elements of schooling, steeplechase, cross-country, long-distance riding and arena jumping before it settled into roughly the format of today. It was years before non-commissioned officers were admitted to international events, and a lot longer before women could take part.

Britain had always entered a team of army officers for the Olympic event, but without any great preparation or special training. When the 10th Duke of Beaufort first introduced the three-day event at Badminton, it was called the 'Olympic Horse Trials' – which was precisely what he intended it to be – but the British Olympic Association took exception to this and the name was soon changed to 'Badminton Three-day Event.'

The evolution of the sport in Britain in just fifty years has been phenomenal. From an activity regarded with some suspicion by the few who knew anything about it, as some sort of continental foible with little appeal to red-blooded Englishmen, it was to become a demanding equestrian discipline at which Britain not only excelled but which it administered so successfully that it was to attract participants from all over the world.

The appeal is not just to the competitors but to all who have an interest in horses and horsemanship. Owners of historic country houses, farmers, National-Trust custodians, and proprietors of riding centres have generously come forward with offers of land – whatever the weather; organisers from every walk of country life have cheerfully taken on the labour of staging the events; thousands more have volunteered their services as officials; and a select but steadily growing band have honed their practical skills as designers and builders of cross-country courses. Except for the directors of the major three-day events, who are now required to give full-time professional service, all are volunteers and upon them the sport is heavily dependent.

Horse trials have become more than a nursery and training ground for international candidates: they are also a booming national sport for many riders who have no aspirations whatsoever to be in a team. And it remains an amateur sport – in spirit, even if a few top riders do manage to make a living out of it. The most successful of riders can find himself suddenly ruled out by some slight unsoundness in his horse and this is sportingly accepted as just another hazard in the game.

Rivalry between competitors and even nations is notably absent, probably because rather than being in direct confrontation with each other they are united in facing the demanding challenges set by the cross-country course designer. Having much in common, they are also good friends in a fairly small world, and such is the spirit of horsemanship that genuine delight is generally shown at the success of other riders, even from opposing teams.

Over the years the type of event horse has changed; a much stronger Thoroughbred element is now being sought. And as the competence of horses and riders has advanced, so has that of the course-designer. Though the required dimensions and the speeds are still the same as they were fifty years ago, it is in the choice of ground, the siting and the combination of the obstacles that the course-designer must keep pace with the rising standard. Much more thought also goes into the convenience and enjoyment of spectators.

Through it all, the welfare of the horse is paramount. It has long been known that the more solid and imposing the fence, the more readily a horse will jump it, but Bill Thomson pioneered fences with quick-release lower rails, in case a horse should become trapped; Frank Weldon delighted in designing fences which might scare the rider while appearing positively inviting to the horse; and considerable effort now goes into improving the ground.

It seems appropriate, on its golden jubilee, to record the development of this sporting phenomenon and to pay tribute to the stalwarts whose enthusiasm, capability and sheer hard work – almost invariably voluntary – brought it about, before they fade altogether from living memory.

Jane Pontifex
October 1998

Olympic Games (48)

Badminton (49-)

Great Auclum (50-55)
Twyford (50-)

Denston Hall (50)
Epperstone (51)
Gisburn (51-56)
Wellesbourne (51-60)

Central Scotland (52-54)
Melton Mowbray (53-58)
Sherborne (53-83)
Shropshire (53)
Stowell Park (53-60)
Tweseldown (53, 54)
Wenlock Edge (53)

Cholmondeley Castle (53-55)
Harewood (53-59)

Coupar Angus (54, 57, 62, 63)

Hovingham (54)
Linlithgow & Stirling (54-56)
Tidworth (54-)
Melton Mowbray (53-58)

Cottesbrooke (55-59)
Fenton (55-85)
Floors Castle (55-75)
Glanusk (55-60)
N.Northumberland (55-57)
Windsor (55)

Callendar (56)
Chatsworth (56-88)
Harringay (56)

Broadhill (57, 58)
Falkirk (57-61)

In 1948 the first post-war Olympic Games were held in London. Organising the equestrian competitions was the responsibility of the newly formed British Horse Society, and the three-day event took place at Aldershot.

There, in an official capacity, was Master, the 10th Duke of Beaufort, who afterwards wrote: 'It seemed to me that this was just the sort of activity for a good English hunter,' and he conceived the idea of running an event at Badminton his Gloucestershire estate: the main purpose being to produce a successful British team for the next Olympics. His friend and neighbour, Colonel Trevor Horn, would organise it, and the BHS would provide financial backing.

Badminton soon established itself as an annual fixture and a major attraction. Today throughout the equestrian world its name is synonymous with the sport, its courses are considered to be more formidable than those of the Olympic Games, and winning it is an almost greater achievement than winning an Olympic gold medal.

In 1951 the Badminton Committee was renamed the Combined Training Committee, and under the Chairmanship of Colonel The Hon Guy Cubitt took on responsibility for regulating the sport on a national basis.

In the early days, many of the competitors were cavalry officers – two of them, Majors Laurence Rook and Frank Weldon, along with Devon farmer Bertie Hill, distinguished themselves in international competitions in the mid-1950s. Hunting also played an important part in the growth of the sport, and held a distinct advantage for the British, both in bringing on riders and in setting standards for cross-country courses.

Most riders competed purely for the fun of it, but there were some with a more professional approach – such as Lt-Colonel Joe Dudgeon, Tony Collings and John Shedden, all of whom understood the baffling mysteries of dressage. Chief among the innovators was Bill Thomson, appointed in 1951 as course-builder and technical advisor to the Combined Training Committee. With his skills as a natural horseman and his ability to design courses which created a positive experience for horses and riders, he was to become a major influence in the sport's development and in the international success of British competitors.

During this first decade the foundations of the sport were further secured with the introduction of one-day events. Originally devised as a preparation for Badminton, they have developed over the years into a nationwide network of competitions, from Pony Club upwards.

One of the few written records of the organisational plans for the Olympic three-day event at Aldershot is a typed list headed 'Equestrian Events – List One'.

From this it appears that apart from the weigh-in scales (with operator), the numbers, telephones and timing equipment, which were to be provided by the Olympic organisers themselves, the entire technical side, personnel and equipment were to be the responsibility of the Institute of the Horse (which, that same year, merged with the National Horse Association to become the British Horse Society). The BHS set up its own committee under Brigadier 'Bogey' Bowden-Smith (one of the few horsemen with experience of actually riding in an Olympic three-day event) and drew heavily upon Army units stationed at Aldershot for the necessary manpower.

The identity of the cross-country course designer is not disclosed, but he made sketches of the fences, with their dimensions, which

Representing Britain (left to right)
Major Douglas Stewart on Dark Seal,
Brigadier Lyndon Bolton (Sylvestre) and
Major Peter Borwick (Liberty).

are reproduced below, exactly as he drew them fifty years later.

The introduction to the final specification of the obstacles reads: 'Height in every case to be measured from ground level, and not to be exceeded in any event. This does not apply to brush fences, that are better left rough to start with and trimmed later to individual directions. Brush fences to be left so that they can be trimmed to a height of 4'6" where required.'

The event ran successfully but there were few spectators – probably because there was hardly anybody in the country at that time who had any idea what a three-day event was or what they could expect to see if they turned up to watch.

Major Borwick, with a fast cross-country, and Brigadier Bolton, with a much superior dressage test, completed the competition well enough, but the team did not finish (only 5 teams out of 14 did) because Major Stewart was eliminated on the steeplechase.

The diagram (*below*) of the show jumping test for the three-day event shows the unusual requirement – on the right hand side – of coming to a halt after jumping fence 4 before turning sharply to retake the same fence as number 5 and continuing on the rest of the track.

Show Jumping Course

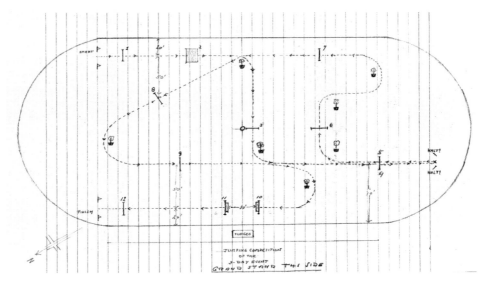

Cross-country Obstacles

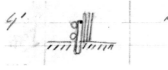

1: Post and 2 rails against bush, rails 3'6", bush 4'.

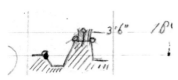

2: Ditch 3' wide x 2' deep, bank 2'6" high, rails and bevins on top, total height 3' 6".

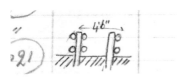

3: Parallel post and rails, 3' 9" high, spaced 4' 6".

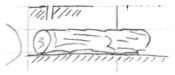

4: Sleeper wall, 3' 9" high.

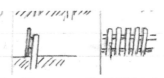

5: Tree-trunk or barrel fence, 3' 6" high.

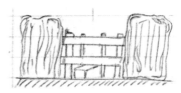

6: Stile 3' 9" high x 6' wide in hedge 6' high.

7: As above, but 24' apart.

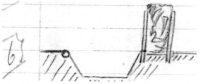

8: Open ditch 6' wide, 3' deep, bush fence 4'.

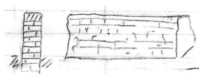

9: Stone wall, 3' 9" high.

10: Post and 3 rails, 3' 6" high, ditch 6' wide, 3' deep.

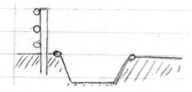

11: Timber-stack, 3' 9" high x 4' spread.

12: Double oxer, rails 3' 6", bush 4', spread 5'.

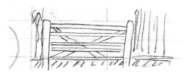

13: Field gate 3' 9" high.

14: Ditch 3' 6" wide x 2' 6" deep, strong bush fence 9' 3" high 2' 6" thick, ditch 3' wide x 3' deep, total spread 10'.

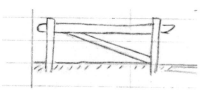

15: Road closed, 3' 6" high.

16: Ditch 4' wide x 3' deep, bank and rails 3' 6"

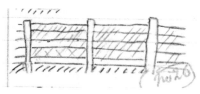

17: Elm-close-boarded fence 3' 9"

18: Bank and rail 3' 6", ditch 4' wide and 3' deep

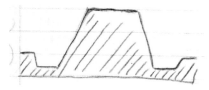

19: Double Irish bank (Please give dimensions).

20: Iron park railings 3' 6" high, hedge behind.

15

21: Timber park fencing 3' 6" at lowest point.

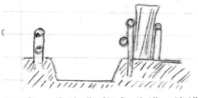

22: Lambing pen, post and rail 3' 6" high, clad corrugated iron.
23: As above, but 30 ft further back then 22.

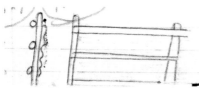

24: Oxrail 2' 6", ditch 4' 6" x 2' 6" deep, post and rail 3' 6", bush 4' high x 2' 6" thick.

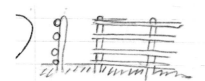

25: Post and rails 3' 9" high.

26: Bush-fence hogs back. Bush 2' 6" high x 2' at 2' bush 3' 9" high x 2', cut bush 2' 6" high x 2', total spread 10'.

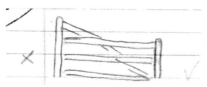

27: Sussex x heave gate 3' 9"

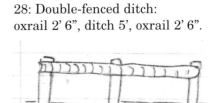

28: Double-fenced ditch: oxrail 2' 6", ditch 5', oxrail 2' 6".

29: Strong single rail 3' 9".

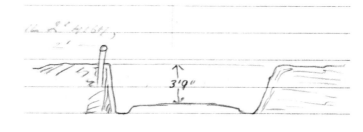

30: Post and rail 3' 6", bush 4' x 2' 6" thick, ditch 4' 6", oxrail 2' 6" .

31, 32: Hollow farm track; oxrail 2' high, drop 3' 9", at 30' rise 3' 9".

33, 34, 35: Reserved for fences particularly suitable to the lie of the land, possibly open water, fence uphill and fence downhill, or a railway crossing

Above: John Shedden on Mrs Home Kidston's Golden Willow, winners of the first Badminton and renowned for flying the Irish Bank on the cross-country course, a leap of some thirty feet.

Right: The Duchess of Beaufort making a presentation to Major Geoffrey Bishop, with Lt-Colonel Trevor Horn looking on. Colonel Horn was the founding organiser. He had help from the Badminton Estate Office and a local secretary, while most of the general secretarial work was done by the BHS in London.

Following the European Championships at Windsor, the spring three-day event returned to Badminton and Lt-Colonel Gordon Cox Cox took over as Director. Our picture shows him escorting the Queen to her Royal Box in a simple grandstand, but there is no formal arena and the spectators are kept back by a single rope. The Queen Mother, Princess Margaret, the Princess Royal (Countess of Harewood) and other members of the Royal Family follow with the Duke of Beaufort, with whom they all stayed at Badminton each year.

It was all delightfully informal by today's standards, but as the crowds inexorably grew each year, more restrictions had to be introduced. Spectators no longer gathered round at the start and finish of Phase D to congratulate the riders as they weighed in, or walked freely on the cross-country course where only the actual obstacles were fenced off with chestnut paling. (It was Colonel Weldon's idea, as Director, to rope off an extended area around each fence, affording the maximum number of spectators a good view.)

Eventually the stables became forbidden territory and the horse inspection was moved from the lovely old stable yard to the gravel sweep in front of Badminton House.

Under the inspiring leadership of its post-war chairman, Colonel The Honourable Guy Cubitt, the Pony Club introduced a Prix Caprilli as an annual inter-branch competition, which in 1949 was held near Newmarket. It was won by the South Berkshire Hunt Branch. (Left to right: Marian Lester, 4th individually; Michael Skinner 2nd to Jane Drummond-Hay; Prudence Knowers, 3rd). Their ponies were owned by the Pullein-Thompsons and trained by them and Henry Wynmalen, formerly from Holland, a distinguished international dressage expert and judge whose all-round equestrian skills and knowledge played an outstanding part in the early development of horse trials.

One of the first one-day events was run at Great Auclum by Neil Gardiner, South Berks Field Master, over fences built by Bill Thomson, Hunt Secretary, and backed by the Army Saddle Club at Camberley, through the good offices of Lt-Colonel Bill Lithgow. Neil Gardiner was a most effective CTC chairman 1951-1966 and was responsible for Bill Thomson's appointment as CTC course-builder.

The obstacles were flimsy by today's standards but natural and well designed.

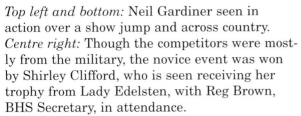

Top left and bottom: Neil Gardiner seen in action over a show jump and across country.
Centre right: Though the competitors were mostly from the military, the novice event was won by Shirley Clifford, who is seen receiving her trophy from Lady Edelsten, with Reg Brown, BHS Secretary, in attendance.
The contretemps graphically illustrated below was thereafter referred to as 'eau de Neil.'

Central Scotland is the oldest one-day event in the calendar and the only one to be still running from the very start. It was organised by Lt-Colonel Mick Lindsay (above left, with Mrs Lindsay) at Hallyburton, his home in Perthshire. For the first couple of years it included roads and tracks. Tony Collings came from Porlock to pass the course and help run the event. The picture at top right is of Cynthia Graham-Menzies, now Mrs Llewellen-Palmer, with her grey mare Melody on the lawn at Hallyburton, in 1950 when the Central Scotland event first started.

Soon after Badminton started, a cable was received at the BHS office in London announcing that a Mr Butler was sending an elephant's tusk as a trophy. The package duly arrived and was unwrapped to reveal a large silver bowl. The first Best British Rider to receive it, at Badminton, was 20-year-old Jane Drummond-Hay riding Happy Knight (2nd). With her is Harry Freeman-Jackson.

After training with Tony Collings at Porlock Vale, Reg Hindley on Speculation, Bertie Hill on Major John Miller's Stella, and Major Laurence Rook on Mrs J.R. Baker's Starlight XV were selected for the team.

Above and left: The team with trainer Tony Collings, (centre) loading up for the flight to Helsinki. For several Olympic Games only one groom per two horses – in whichever discipline – was allowed in the official team, and it took strong pressure from the FEI to increase this to one groom per horse.

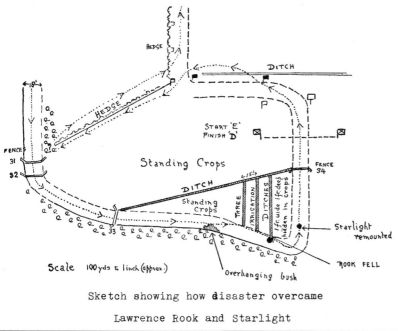

Scale   100 yds = 1 inch (approx.)

Sketch showing how disaster overcame

Lawrence Rook and Starlight

Unfortunately, near the end of the course, Starlight put his foot in a hole and threw his rider who, though concussed, managed to remount. After jumping the final fence (seen above) he crossed the line outside the finishing flag and was eliminated. The sketchmap on left, drawn by an anonymous onlooker, charts the disaster.

The first European champion was Major Laurence Rook on Starlight XV (*opposite*), who achieved maximum bonus marks (awarded for time within the time allowed) on the speed and endurance. In the other picture he is watched by The Queen and Princess Margaret (in mourning for the late King George VI), with Prince Philip and the Duke and Duchess of Beaufort. The Duke used to drive them round the course, where they either watched the more interesting fences from strategically placed wagons or simply mingled with the crowds of spectators.

Below: The victorious British team of Major Frank Weldon on Kilbarry (second overall, medals had not yet been introduced), Reg Hindley on Speculation and Bertie Hill on Margaret Hough's Bambi V. Britain was the first country to establish a regular annual three-day event and so had been invited by the FEI to host the initial European Championships. Switzerland and Ireland also entered teams but failed to finish with all three riders. Sweden, France and Holland sent individual entries. Badminton did not stage the championships again, because its April date was too early for the continental teams to get their horses fit: their winter training being largely confined to indoor school work. Among other competitors that year were Brigadier Lyndon Bolton, Major Dick Hern, Diana Mason, Brian Young, Cherrie Kendall and Major Bill Lithgow.

The Army originally ran an autumn one-day event at Tweseldown Racecourse, where the central mound was built on Queen Victoria's orders for reviewing her troops; the Queen's Room is still in the buildings (below left). Below right are the management committee, who now run all events here under a MoD lease, including the first three-day event held on the site since the Olympic Games in 1948 (see pages 13 to 16).

Sherborne Castle, Dorset, built by Sir Walter Raleigh in 1594, has been the home of the Digby family since 1617. The horse trials were run by the Blackmore and Sparkford Vale Hunt.

Dressage and show jumping took place below the castle, and the cross-country course ran over the steep slopes of the deer park to finish back on the flat ground below.

Right: Guy Dawson, agent to the Sherborne estate, with Roy Lewis, in charge of dressage and show jumping, and Lt-Colonel Gavin Young (on shooting-stick) organiser of the event.

29

Tony Collings, pioneer of horse trials in Britain after the war, trained the 1952 Olympic team at his Porlock Vale riding centre (below, with Laurence Rook and Reg Hindley).

Since his death in the 1954 Comet crash, a trophy (above) showing him winning Badminton 1950 on Remus has been awarded annually to the rider gaining most points.

The Combined Training Committee at a meeting at 16 Bedford Square during the 1950s (seated, clockwise from left): Colonel Sandie Monroe, from Scotland; Colonel The Honourable Guy Cubitt, first Chairman and elder statesman of the sport; Reg Hindley, Olympic competitor and Director of Harewood; the Duke of Beaufort; Brigadier P.E. ('Bogey') Bowden-Smith, competitor in the 1924 Paris Olympics and Chairman of the selection committee; Colonel Trevor Horn, first Director of Badminton; Major Frank Weldon, team captain; Lieut. Colonel Gordon Cox Cox, second Director of Badminton; Neil Gardiner, Chairman, organiser of Great Auclum Horse Trials; Colonel Mike Ansell, BHS Director; Colonel Vivian ('Pudding') Williams, Chairman of the Dressage Committee, distinguished dressage judge and trainer and owner of several three-day event horses; Colonel R.B. ('Babe') Moseley, Badminton's first Assistant Director, first BHS steward and, later, Chairman of the Junior selection committee: Ted Marsh; Charles Cornell, BHS Treasurer.

(Standing, left to right): Colonel Charles Adderley, BHS Assistant Director, who oversaw combined training; Bill Thomson, first Technical Adviser, course designer of Harewood, Burghley and many other events; Reg Brown, BHS Secretary.

The second European Three-Day Event Championships were organised by the Swiss, and though the course, made treacherous by heavy rain, was particularly difficult, the British team (left) of Major Frank Weldon, Bertie Hill, Laurence Rook and Diana Mason won the gold by nearly 600 points from Germany. No other team completed. The British also won all three individual medals: Bertie Hill (gold) on Ted Marsh's Crispin (below at home in Devon), Frank Weldon (silver) on Kilbarry and Laurence Rook (bronze) on Starlight XV.

At Basle, teams of four, with the best three scores to count, were admitted for the first time. Diana Mason (*below, left*) was the first lady to be selected for a British team. Although hers was the discard score, she finished seventh overall and performed the best dressage test on her little mare Tramella. With her are Laurence Rook, Frank Weldon and Margaret Hough, who rode as an individual and came sixth on her Badminton winner Bambi V.

Left: Frank Weldon, British team captain and silver medallist, rides Kilbarry in the dressage.

Always a keen spectator at Badminton, the Queen invited the 1955 European Championships to Windsor. Britain's Frank Weldon, Bertie Hill and Laurence Rook (left) won the team championship, Frank Weldon (above, on Kilbarry) won the individual gold medal, Lt-Commander John Oram (opposite, above, on Radar) the silver, and Bertie Hill the bronze. *Opposite, below:* Bertie gives his prize back to the Queen, owner of the great Countryman, with the words 'I think this is yours, Ma'am'.

This highly popular pre-Badminton event, which ran for thirty years, was organised on behalf of the North Northumberland Hunt by Lord and Lady Joicey at Lord Lambton's estate in the untrammelled countryside between the Scottish Borders and the Cheviots. Michael Joicey oversaw the cross-country and his wife Elisabeth was secretary for 19 years, until the farming situation in the park at Fenton restricted the room available for a good course.

Lady Joicey writes: 'Fenton was famous for icy, usually snowy, weather during March and early April, when up here it is grey, windy, sleety and bitterly cold.

'In the '50s and early '60s many of the local foxhunters used to keep their horses up an extra week or two and have a ride round Fenton.

'My mother was famous for a remark about a lady who was probably ahead of her time in dressage and always rode very well-schooled horses. "I rather hope that so-and-so does not win", said my mother. "She is always practising, and it IS so unfair" and, in those days, so it was!'

Opposite, below: Early committee members (left to right) Michael and Elisabeth Joicey, Austin Kirkup, Alice Benson, Horace Davidson and Howard Phillips.
Above: Lucinda Lambton presenting a prize to Elisabeth Joicey.

Right: Northumberland-born Duncan Burns of Midland Bank, major sponsors of one-day events from 1969 to 1985. As the Bank's horse trials co-ordinator he presided over hundreds of prize-givings, in fair weather and foul, often as the light was fading and sometimes illuminated by motorcar headlights.

The steep grounds of the Duke of Devonshire's home in theDerbyshire Peak District overlooking the River Derwent gave tremendous scope for a cross-country course, which included such dramatic water jumps as Queen Mary's Bower and the Ice Pond.

Chatsworth staged the first Midland Bank Championships (Novice) in 1969. In 1984 it up-graded and ran as an autumn three-day event until 1989, when heavy rain damaged the park.

Below: The course plan from the first programme.

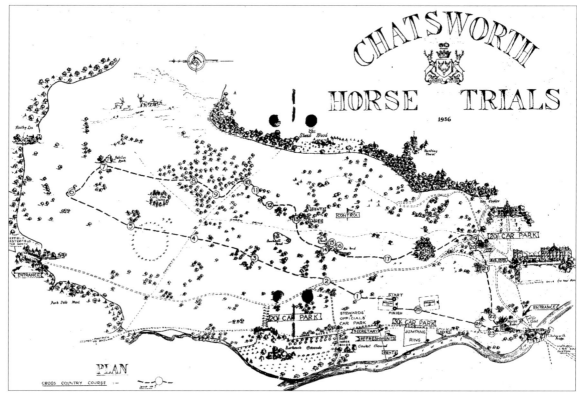

The 1956 Olympic Games were held in Melbourne, Australia, but because of the stringent quarantine requirements and the problems of long-distance travel for the horses, the equestrian events were held in Stockholm.

Below: The British team – Colonel Frank Weldon, Major Laurence Rook and Bertie Hill – won the gold medal from Germany (silver), Canada (bronze) and 16 other teams.

Right: Frank Weldon won the individual bronze.

Previous page: Even in those days there were 'photo calls'. Here Frank Weldon and Bertie Hill are shown 'schooling' at Badminton before they set off for Stockholm.

Opposite page, above: The team with their horses – Laurence Rook with Ted Marsh's Wild Venture, Bertie Hill with the Queen's Countryman and Frank Weldon with Kilbarry.

Opposite, below: The three gold medallists with leading show jumper Pat Smythe and Colonel Arthur Main, BHS and Coaching Club Chairman, after they had all received BHS gold medals.

Britain's gold medal team in training at Windsor (left to right): Ted Marsh, Frank Weldon (non-competing captain), Derek Allhusen, Kit Tatham-Warter, Sheila Willcox and Gillian Morrison (individual). *Opposite page:* Second after the dressage – a very quiet affair, as our picture shows – Sheila went into the lead after the cross-country (*top*) and became the first European lady champion.

Buccleuch (58-60)
Harrogate (58-)
Sand Farm (58)
Scone Palace (58-61)
Tetbury (58-60)
Tetcott (58)
Tidworth (58-)
WardenLaw (58)

Catterick (59, 60, 65, 66)
Crawley&Horsham (59, 60)
Durham (59)
Eglinton (59-)
Somerset (59)
Tiverton (59)

Dunster (60, 61)

Powderham (60,61,63,65-74,
    77, 79-83, 87-96, 98-)
Southill (60, 62, 63)

Burghley (61-)
Edenbridge (61-64)
Edinburgh (61-73)
Hampshire (61)
Lichfield (61-64)
Solihull (61)
Sussex (61)
Upton House (61, 62)

Aughton (62, 63)
Burley on the Hill (62, 63)
Cirencester (62)
Coldstream (62-68)
Crookham (62-92)
Eridge (62-72)
Everdon (62-)
Stokenchurch (62-79)
Wetherby (62, 63)
Wylye (62-90)

Downlands (Liphook) (63-82)
Lanark (63-67)

Aberuthven (64-79)
Kinlet (64-78)
Louth (64-67)
Wakefield (64-68, 82)

Benenden (65, 66)
Hereford (65)
Mixbury (65, 66, 68)
Papplewick (65-68)

Bretherton (66, 68-70)
Droitwich (66, 67)
Kemsing (66)

Birkhill (67, 68)
Cullompton (67-71)
Overstone (67)
Stoneleigh (67-80)

There were no European Championships in 1958, but Britain was appointed to run them in 1959 at the Yorkshire home of the Earl of Harewood and the Princess Royal (Princess Mary). Ten nations sent teams, including three from behind the Iron Curtain: Poland, USSR and Bulgaria. They caused a great stir and all three finished.

The following spring brought the first Australians to compete in Britain, as preparation for the Olympic Games in Rome. Bill Roycroft, already in his 50s, won Badminton on the 15hh Our Solo and Laurie Morgan was second on Salad Days. They went on to win team gold and individual gold and silver in Rome.

This decade saw the inauguration of Burghley Horse Trials, under the inspiring direction of James Grose, replacing Harewood as the main autumn three-day event. As CT Field Director also, Brigadier Grose introduced horse registration (10/-) and CT Group membership (5/-) within the BHS membership, to raise the sport's regular income.

Burghley hosted the European Championships in 1962 and the first World Championships in 1966 – despite the banning of all horses from Europe, due to an outbreak of African Horse Sickness, which reduced teams to the statutory minimum (5).

The downgrading of Badminton to a one-day event in 1963, because of bad weather, meant a worrying financial setback. Neil Gardiner resigned as chairman and BHS chairman Bill Barton took over until the appointment of Colonel Gordon Cox Cox, who had been director of Badminton committee as course-designer and subsequently took over also as director.

The Tokyo Olympics of 1964 were the first in which lady riders were allowed to compete (Lana Dupont rode there for the USA). The British team was eliminated.

In 1967 a number of new lady riders came to the fore, but it was an all-male team that carried off the European gold medal at Punchestown – where show jumping in reverse order of placing was tried out for the first time.

Also in 1967, the first Junior European Championships took place at Eridge, in Sussex, largely at the instigation of Colonel 'Babe' Moseley. There were not enough nations for a team classification but the French riders, under the direction of their trainer, Jack Le Goff, won both the individual gold and bronze .

When the BHS office moved from London to Stoneleigh, Jane Pontifex who had been Horse Trials Secretary since 1949 resigned – though she continued to score at many of the major events – and was succeeded by Eileen Thomas, former Pony Club Secretary and also an experienced scorer.

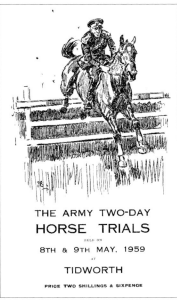

THE ARMY TWO-DAY
HORSE TRIALS
HELD ON
8TH & 9TH MAY, 1959
AT
TIDWORTH
PRICE **TWO** SHILLINGS & SIXPENCE

Top right: Preparing for the horse inspection on the Fisher polo ground.

With armoured (cavalry) divisions stationed at Tidworth, the Army Saddle Club ran first one-day, then two-day and then, for 19 years, three-day events. It always featured a Military section (prizewinners on the occasion *below* including Captain Mark Phillips, Princess Anne and Captain Malcolm Wallace) and later added the National Junior Championship.

Sheila Willcox established a record in winning Badminton three years running which will probably never be equalled. Others have won the great three-day event more often, but not in successive years.

With her part-Highland dun gelding High and Mighty (*left*), Sheila was a perfectionist in dressage, and in 1955 the pair won in Turin, where she was the first lady rider to lead an international event in both dressage and cross-country. Second to Frank Weldon on her first appearance at Badminton in 1956, she went on to win Harewood that autumn, then won Badminton for the next two years with High and Mighty and (by now Mrs Waddington) a third time in 1959 with Airs and Graces (*below*).

The European Championships, with a record ten teams taking part, was the culmination of seven years of three-day events at the Yorkshire home of the Earl of Harewood and the Princess Royal (Princess Mary), who is seen here presenting the individual gold medal to Captain Hans Schwarzenbach (Switzerland) on Burn Trout – bought from Colonel Frank Weldon, who was second on Samuel Johnson.

47

Eglinton is one of the longest-running events of all and it has been organised throughout by The Honourable Heather Galbraith – though the whole family is always involved – at Lord Strathclyde's Barskimming, Mauchline, their home in Ayrshire. The three generations on the left are Heather – in riding gear, as she was a regular competitor in those days and rode in the first Eglinton event – her mother, Lady Strathclyde and niece Ghislaine Galbraith.

Below: Lorna Alexander (wearing headphones) with her team at cross-country control. This is an arduous job regularly undertaken by Mrs Alexander at various Scottish events, where her husband Ronald is generally either course-designer or technical adviser.

Right: Forty years on.
At a special celebration party in 1998, Horse Trials Director Major Tim Taylor presented Heather with honorary life membership of the BHTA (British Horse Trials Association), to mark her four decades as organiser of the Eglinton event.

Below: The water splash on Eglinton's attractive cross-country course, built mainly on Highaird Farm, in a bend in the River Ayr. There is an assortment of drop fences on the steep descent through trees to the water meadow and an uphill climb back to the central area.

The Rome Olympic Games were held at Pratoni del Vivaro, in a spectacular rural setting south of the city.

The British team in training under the captaincy of Colonel Frank Weldon (*on the left*) were Michael Cavenagh, Bertie Hill, Captain Norman Arthur, Michael Bullen and Jeremy Smith-Bingham. Wel-

don, Hill, Arthur and Bullen were selected.

On cross-country day Bertie Hill, suffering from raging toothache, made a nonsense of Phase E, the run-in, and on the last day Norman Arthur's horse (Ted Marsh's Blue Jeans) was withdrawn. The other three all jumped clear, losing the

team bronze medal to France by only half a mark. Michael Bullen finished fourth on Colonel and Mrs V.D.S. Williams's grey mare, Cottage Romance.

In the French team was Jack le Goff, who finished in sixth place. Anton Bühler from Switzerland won the bronze medal.

The Australian campaign for the Olympic Games in Rome proved to be well worth the effort. Bill Roycroft won at Badminton in the spring on Our Solo, Laurie Morgan was second on Salad Days and Neale Lavis fourth on Mirrabooka. In Rome it was Laurie Morgan who took the individual gold medal, Neale Lavis the silver, and these two, plus Bill Roycroft (Our Solo) and Brian Crago (Sabre) won the team championships by more than 250 points from Switzerland. The team then went home to Australia but Laurie stayed in Britain, to win Badminton with Salad Days in 1961.

28 riders compete at Powderham

TWENTY-EIGHT riders—some from as far away as the Midlands, Kent, and Monmouthshire—competed yesterday in the first Powderham Castle preliminary horse trials, an event which is almost certain to become one of the most important in the Westcountry's riding calendar.

Originally there were 42 entries for the trials, but these were reduced to 28 through last-minute lameness and through the current outbreak of coughing among horses.

Even so the trials were such a success that it seems likely that next year they will also include intermediate events. The perfect setting of Powderham Park was the main reason for the success.

One of the best crosscountry courses in Devon had been built for the event. Just over two and a half miles long, the course wound its way around Powderham Castle itself and included water jumps and a testing quarry section.

20 sets of jumps

The trials, which were run under British Horse Society rules, were won by Miss S. Whitmore, of Kent, with Miss R. Wylie, of Langport, Somerset, second, and Miss J.

Powderham Castle, which lies on the western bank of the Exe estuary not far from Exeter, was built at the end of the 14th century by Sir Philip Courtenay. Damaged during the Civil War, it was later restored and much of the original structure can still be seen.

The annual horse trials, held in the deer park, were initiated by the Earl and Countess of Devon, and are now run by their son and daughter-in-law, Lord and Lady Courtenay. The whole family is involved, from Lord Courtenay himself – seen (*opposite, top*) supervising a fence repair by Major Michael Strachan and Graham Miles, and the safe extraction of a horse cast in a ditch – to daughter Camilla, creosoting a fence with girl grooms Christelle Minchin and Sharon Crook. The Royal Devon Yeomanry are in charge of communications on cross-country day. The Courtenays also run many Pony Club events at Powderham.

The successful European Championships of 1959 brought Harewood to a close. As Britain was due to run the championships again in 1962, a replacement was urgently needed, and the search ended at Burghley, historic Elizabethan seat of the Marquess of Exeter.

Opposite page
Far left: Lord Exeter.
Above: Brigadier James Grose, Burghley organiser, and field director of horse trials and dressage, with secretaries Sarah Glyn, Michelle Asa-Thomas and Jill Neill.

The dressage arena *(top)* and Trout Hatchery (centre, and left, tackled by Frank Weldon) as they were in 1961.
Right: Janine Sebag-Montefiore and Samantha at Capability's Cutting.

The only stud in this country to have been devoted to the production of event horses is the Welton Stud, run by Sam Barr and his wife Linda at their Limbury Farm, Gloucestershire. Welton Gameful was the foundation stallion – *above, left,* as a yearling – by Prince's Game (by Dastur) out of Welton (by Philae Pharos Phalaris), bought by Sam as a foal in 1961. To the right of Gameful is Louis, his first foal to be kept entire, sire of

European champion Welton Romance; below them, Sam rides Gameful's first foal, the gelding Gamekeeper.

Sam always hunted but only took up eventing at the age of 50. His daughter Dawn is riding Gameful (this page, *above*) at Tidworth in 1971 to qualify as a Junior.

The name Welton has become familiar throughout the eventing world, many of the dynasty competing as entires. Sam is breeding now for more blood – especially with weights no longer to be carried – and seven-eighths is average. With him and Linda (*right*) is their latest foal, by Welton Crackerjack out of an imported New Zealand mare.

A fter just one year's experience, Burghley took on
the running of the European
Championships in which
teams from France, Ireland
and the USSR were entered.
As well as a team, Britain
fielded nine individuals (this
was before additional entries
from the host nation were
restricted to two 'official' plus
six more individuals). A few
days before the champi-
onships opened, the huge
Russian lorries which had
driven all the way from
Moscow turned in through
the stable gates off the
Barnack Road and the
horses stumbled out under
the arc lights to snuff the
night air and fall upon the
fresh grass. Their legs had
filled enormously on the long
journey, but they recovered
remarkably quickly and won
the team gold medal by a
comfortable margin from
Ireland.

The British team consisting of Frank Weldon riding Young Pretender, Michael Bullen (Sea Breeze), Susan Fleet (The Gladiator) and Peter Welch (Mister Wilson) won the bronze medal, and it was another British rider, Captain James Templer, RHA, who carried off the individual gold, riding his own M'Lord Connolly (*right and opposite*). Two years later they won at Badminton. Another British individual, Jane Wykeham-Musgrave (*below*) on her own Ryebrooks, 'the best friend I ever had', lost her cross-country lead with an expensive show jumping round, but still won the bronze medal, behind German (*sic*) Gazumov (USSR) on Granj.

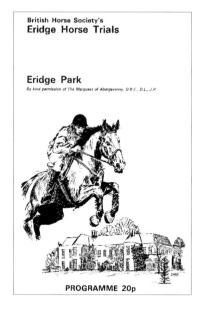

British Horse Society's
Eridge Horse Trials

Eridge Park
By kind permission of The Marquess of Abergavenny, O.B.E., D.L., J.P.

PROGRAMME 20p

For ten years the opening autumn one-day event was run at Eridge Park, the East Sussex home of the Marquess of Abergavenny, before hosting the first European Junior Championships. In 1994 it returned as a one-day event.

Below: Scorers at work (left to right) Jane Pontifex, Eileen Thomas and Jane Dewey, with help from Sheila Willcox (standing).

Crookham ran as an early spring event for more than 30 years, organised first by Mrs Peggy Maxwell, then by John Stevens, and finally by Mrs Sally Bullen. It took place on Tweseldown Racecourse, near Aldershot, but was named after the nearby village of Crookham to distinguish it from the autumn event. Tweseldown was a cold, bleak venue and the event was sometimes in danger of cancellation – or was actually cancelled – due to snow, as shown below. Sally is seen discussing the prospects with technical adviser Noel Palmer.

Above: Michael Bullen riding in a veterans class across Tweseldown's central hilltop overlooking the cross-country course.

Below: John Tulloch, Chairman, presenting Sally Bullen with her Horse Trials Award in 1991, after 22 years as organiser.

Above: Lord Hugh Russell on the attractive cross-country course at the Northamptonshire event which ran for 35 years.

Below: Captain Tadzik Kopanski and Plain Sailing, later sold to the USA and medallist in two Olympics and a World Championship.

Captain Dick Hawkins, host and organiser, on his hunter Corky.

F or 23 years Lord and Lady Hugh Russell ran horse trials over the steep slopes of their land on the edge of Salisbury Plain – first one-day and then international three-day events. Hugh served on the Horse Trials Committee, as a steward and as Chairman of selectors, and Rosemary was an outstanding cross-country trainer to the British team who used to assemble for their final concentration at Wylye. After her hunting fall in 1967, she became famous for directing operations from her Minimoke.

Kenneth and Hester Poland owned the land at Downlands and Woolmer Farm, near Liphook in Hampshire, where Mrs Poland, a keen horse trials supporter, organised one of the most successful pre-Badminton spring events. The course ran over open fields and down through trees into the steep river valley, where the obstacles included a spectacular leap over the stream at the bottom of the hill. *Top right:* Two of the woodmen whose skills were invaluable.

Patience Minister of the West Norfolk branch (*above*) winner of the first under-18 Individual Championship which was added to the Team Championship in 1963 and held at Burghley. *Below*: From left to right, prize winners, Peggy Carey, Patience Minister and Judith Garrard.

Above: The Marquess of Exeter, between Brigadier James Grose, Burghley Director, and Sir Henry Tate, Chairman.

65

Kinlet Hall, Moffat's Preparatory School in Shropshire, has always featured equestrian activities and Pony Club events. In the '60s and '70s it held a series of excellent horse trials over its open parkland with some steep gradients.

The event was organised by joint-headmaster David Engleheart *(below)* and his wife Esmé *(left,* with Colonel Henry Nicoll who designed the course). 'He was a genius course-designer', says David, 'and Esmé did the work. I just did the talking.'

The USSR staged its first European Championships at Moscow. In addition to the host nation, there were three teams entered from eastern Europe and three, including Britain, from the west.

The British team – with Colonel Bill Lithgow as chef d'équipe for the first time – put up a consistent performance to take the bronze medal, not far behind Ireland (silver) and the USSR (gold), while the sole individual rider, Mary Macdonell on Kilmacthomas, finished a good fourth.

Among the supporters who travelled to Moscow with the team was Colonel Babe Moseley *(right)*, chairman of the selectors. He took great exception to the restrictions of the communist regime and one evening, convinced that his hotel room must be bugged, sat on his bed and loudly voiced his objections – then felt much better.

Left to right: Richard Meade with Barberry, Christine Sheppard (Fenjirao), Mary Macdonell (Kilmacthomas), Derek Allhusen (Lochnivar) and Ben Jones (Master Bernard).

Burghley's reputation for first-class organisation was recognised when the FEI chose it as venue for the first World Championships. As the date drew nearer, a virulent epidemic of African Horse Sickness spread through Europe, and the Ministry of Agriculture imposed a total ban on horses travelling from the Continent. However, with Britain plus Ireland, and the USA, who transported their horses by air, Argentina, who brought theirs by sea, and the USSR

who doggedly drove the whole way across Europe without ever letting the horses out of the lorry, the statutory minimum of five teams was achieved.

The result was an overwhelming victory for the Irish team by a margin of just under 300. *Opposite* The winning team: Major Eddie Boylan on Durlas Eile, Penelope Moreton on Loughlin, Virginia Freeman-Jackson on Sam Weller and Tommy Brennan on Kilkenny. In the '90s, Tommy has been cross-country designer at Punchestown. Kilkenny was sold to Jimmy Wofford (they won team silver for the USA in Mexico and Munich Olympics.)

Argentina won the silver, but neither Britain nor the other three teams finished the competition intact.

The individual gold medal was won by Argentina's Captain Carlos Moratorio on Chalan, silver medallist in 1964. Richard Meade on Barberry (*above*) took the silver, and Virginia Freeman-Jackson with her little Sam Weller held off Eddie Boylan for the bronze by one-tenth of a point. Seven of Britain's 13 individual runners completed the event.

Marian Eason riding her mare Alitza (above) over a fence in front of Overstone School near Northampton. *Right:* Event organiser Colonel Tom Greenhalgh with Anneli Drummond-Hay, who rode his horse Merely-a-Monarch in an outstanding career which included winning Burghley in 1961 and Badminton in 1962, before going on to international honours in show jumping. Tom Greenhalgh was a generous but unobtrusive supporter of horse trials, raising sponsorship for teams and riders; he was also one of the founders of the Horse Trials Support Group.

Only Britain and France entered for the first European Junior Championships at Eridge, the Marquess of Abergavenny's estate in Sussex, so there was no team championship. The individual championship was a runaway victory for Alain Souchon of France, who rode an outstanding dressage test on Roi d'Asturie. The silver medal was won by Richard Walker (*above*) on his own Pasha.

Left: Richard in South Africa, before his family moved to Britain in 1961.

71

Ireland's first international championship was a tough one. Britain's team (left to right) Major Derek Allhusen riding Lochnivar, Richard Meade on Barberry, Martin Whiteley (The Poacher) and Sergeant Ben Jones (Foxdor) won the gold medal from Ireland, whose Major Eddie Boylan took the individual gold on his 1965 Badminton winner, Durlas Eile. Martin Whiteley (*above*) won individual silver and Derek Allhusen bronze.

Back-trouble put a stop to Martin's career, but he lent his brilliant horse The Poacher for other team riders and he himself became a Combined Training Committee member and eventually its chairman, also chairman of the selection committee. He was the main founder, and first chairman, of the Horse Trials Support Group until his untimely death in 1984.

Batsford (68 - 88)
Everingham (68 - 73)
Farleigh (68 - 77)
Windsor (68 -)
Wingerworth (68 - 70, 72,73, 76 - 84)

Annick (69 - 82)
Burgess Hill (69, 70)
Galashiels (69 - 72)
Hawley (69 - 75)
Kirtlington (69)
Lockerbie (69 - 82)
Osberton (69 - 71, 73 - 77, 80 -)

Assington (70 - 72)
Brigstock (70 - 98)
Caldwell (70 - 80)
Coombe Bisset (70 - 74)
Cropwell Bishop (70 -72)
Kilsby (70 - 74, 80)
Knowlton (70, 72, 77, 79)
Kyre (70 - 82)
Rushall (70 - 85)
Scofton (70)
St Ives (70)

Backwell (71)
Bucklebury (71 - 84)
Chagford (71 - 84)
Cirencester (72 - 75)
Corbridge (71 - 80)
Elleron (71, 72)
Ermington (71 - 89)
Forest Mere (Stocklands) (71 - 74)
Goodwood (71 - 83)

Graveley (71 -)
Holme Lacey (71, 72)
Ickworth Park (71 - 73, 83 - 95)
Malpas (71 - 74)
Meldon (71)
Penzance (71 -)
Wing (71 - 73)

Llanfechain (72 -)
Meriden (72 - 79)
Sion Park (72)
South Warnborough (72)
Taunton (72 -)

Bramham (73 -)
Claughton (73 - 89)
Dauntsey Park (73 -)
East Hanningfield (73 -77)
Henstridge (73 - 79)

Ingleden Park (73, 74, 76, 77)
Ledstone (73)
Molland (73 - 93)
Royal Welsh (73 - 90)
Weston Park (73 -)
Weymouth (73 - 80)
Strathendrick (73, 74)
Tranwell (Morpeth) (73, 74)
Wendover (73 - 76, 80 - 85)

Charnock Richard (74)
Royal Lancs (74)
Warfield (74)

Devonshaw (75 - 80)
Earl Soham (75 - 83)
Firle Place (75 -)

Lockerley Hall (75 - 78)
Locko Park (75 - 91)
Margam Park (Penrice) (75 -83)
Pembroke (76 - 79)
Solihull (75, 83 -)
South of England (75 -)
Tatton Park (75, 76)
Wramplingham (75 - 87)

Billesdon (76 - 82)
Bolton (76)
Brougham (76 -)
Charterhall (76 -)
Coakham (76, 77)
Cromer (76)
Pollok Park (76)
Portman (76 -)
Royal Deeside (76 -)
Rudding Park (76 - 88)
Sandhurst (76)
Vale of York (76 - 78)
Wilton (76 -)

Aston Park (77 - 95)
Bicton (77 -)
Burgie (77 -)
Chilham Castle (77 - 92)
Frensham (77 - 85)
Great Missenden (77 -)
Rufford Park (77 - 82)
Scunthorpe (77 -)
Suckley (77 - 82)
Tetbury (77 - 92)
Winkfield (77)

In an unprecedented run of continuous success each year from 1968 to 1972, British teams won gold medals at every international championship, as well as individual golds in 1970, 1971 and 1972.

Two major boosts to the sport during this period were the appearance of Midland Bank as sponsors and of Princess Anne as a competitor. The Bank, discreet and undemanding, were to invest a huge amount of time and money during the years from 1968 to 1985, providing prize money for most of the one-day and some of the more recent three-day events.

The support of HM The Queen had been invaluable, and the arrival of her daughter on the scene as a competitor provided further encouragement. The Princess was a first-class horsewoman and needed no favours to establish herself among the top event riders – delighting everyone with her individual gold medal in the 1971 European Championships.

In 1973, Britain's senior team (in which Lucinda Prior-Palmer made her debut on the first of her six Badminton winners, Be Fair) battled it out for team bronze over the notorious course at the European Championships in Kiev – where Janet Hodgson received a special award for her courage in completing the competition despite injuring her face badly in a fall. Meanwhile, Virginia Holgate was making her first appearance at an international competition, winning the European Junior Championships at Pompadour, in France.

In 1974 at Burghley came a serious challenge to British dominance. The Americans, who had been hard on Britain's heels since Jack Le Goff's appointment as their trainer in 1971, became World Champions and also won individual gold.

At home, James Grose was succeeded by Lt-Colonel Peter Hodgson as Horse Trials Director, but he continued as Director of Burghley until 1976, when he was succeeded by Major Andrew Burnaby-Atkins. Laurence Rook became Chairman of the CTC and John Anderson joined Bill Thomson as a technical adviser.

In 1972 Eileen Thomas left the BHS, but continued to work as a freelance entries secretary and scorer until moving in 1974 to the USA at the invitation of Neil Ayer. As Combined Training Executive Director for the next 17 years, she set up the infrastructure of the USCTA, based on that of horse trials in Britain, and introduced the British 'instant scoring' system.

Eileen's place at Stoneleigh was filled by Nici Gibb, while Jean Sansome (dressage executive) took on a share of responsibility for Combined Training. Nici left five years later to live in the Border Country, scoring for many of the Scottish events and returning south each year to score at Badminton. By this time the administration of the sport had expanded so much that the work was divided between various departments and the Executive Secretary role disappeared.

It was Mrs Jacquie Mason who, having set up in business in the early '70s, first as an entries secretary and then as a scorer, introduced computer scoring. With the technical help of Paul Harris, she has continued to refine and modernise the system. From the very beginning, Britain has set the pattern and led the world in this vital aspect of organisation.

In 1971 Osberton expanded into a three-day event, and in 1974 Bramham followed suit. In 1975 Badminton was abandoned to the rain after two days of dressage, with Lucinda Prior-Palmer in the lead.

The following year (1976), Lucinda won her second Badminton on Mrs Vicky Phillips's Wideawake – who, to the horror of the crowd, on his lap of honour collapsed and died in the arena. That same summer in Montreal the Olympic Games brought further misfortune for Lucinda, when Be Fair broke down on the cross-country – as did Hugh Thomas's Playamar – and the team failed to finish.

In 1977 there was consolation for Lucinda when she won her third Badminton with Mrs Elaine Straker's George – on whom she went on to win the European Championships at Burghley. Later that same year she obtained the first commercial sponsorship of any rider.

During this decade, as the domestic sport expanded it became necessary to bring in or tighten up a number of administrative arrangements and regulations. CT Group horse registration fees were increased to £2 and entry fees to £4. Omnibus schedules – as opposed to separate schedules produced by each organiser – were introduced, but met a good deal of opposition from organisers because of the proposed charge of £25. A recommendation that all entries should be centralised in the CT Office was turned down as too costly and labour-intensive – also because most organisers wished to retain control of their own entries.

The first ballot system was introduced, to accommodate as fairly as possible the number of entries that could not be accepted at oversubscribed events. Because of the problem of late withdrawals, riders would be required to produce a veterinary certificate for a second offence, under penalty of automatic suspension for three months.

Princess Anne started competing in official horse
trials with Purple Star,
whose dam Stella was event-
ed by the Crown Equerry, Sir
John Miller, and lent by him
for Bertie Hill to ride in the
Helsinki Olympics in 1952.
In 1968 Princess Anne competed at Eridge, where she is
seen watching the cross-
country with the Queen and
with her trainer, Alison
Oliver (left).

B atsford Park in the Cotswolds, home of Lord Dulverton, was the delightful setting for the event run by the Heythrop Hunt and Evenlode Riding Club.

Held on the Hely-Hutchinsons' land at Farleigh Castle – family home of Pollyann Lochore (née Hely-Hutchinson) – the cross-country course ran through the park and the dressage took place in front of Farleigh House boys' preparatory school (*left*). The event was organised by Mrs Bridget Parker who, like so many riders, turned to organisation and other official duties on retirement from competition.

Right and below: Richard Walker and his brilliant little chestnut Pasha won the individual gold with a score of one penalty point.

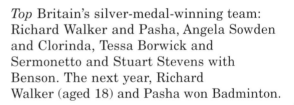

Top Britain's silver-medal-winning team: Richard Walker and Pasha, Angela Sowden and Clorinda, Tessa Borwick and Sermonetto and Stuart Stevens with Benson. The next year, Richard Walker (aged 18) and Pasha won Badminton.

J ane Bullen, Richard Meade, Staff Sergeant Ben Jones from The King's Troop RHA and Mark Phillips (reserve) embarking for Mexico. Dressage rider Jook Hall (holding hat) travelled with them, her husband Robert having flown ahead with their horse, Conversano Caprice.

Above: The victorious British riders displaying their team gold. On left is Derek Allhusen with the individual silver – won after one of the most arduous three-day events ever. Dry heat was followed by torrential rain and flash floods, forcing later competitors to swim rather than jump the water obstacles.

Jane Bullen, dismounted, on a steep stretch of roads and tracks nearly lost Our Nobby, but caught his tail and was hauled to the top.

Right: A nosebag for Major Derek Allhusen's Lochinvar at a celebration lunch in London.

First a one-day, then a two-day event, Osberton ran for many years, up to 1998, as an intermediate three-day event, organised by Michael Foljambe at his home in Nottinghamshire. In the event's latter years it ran a special class for aspiring Young Riders, whose Chairman, Christopher Schofield (*left*) is seen inspecting the course with Major Tim Taylor.

The first Midland Bank Novice Champion-ship, won by Sarah Roger-Smith (*below*), was held at Chatsworth, where the Queen, accompanied by the Duchess of Devonshire, presented the prizes. The River Derwent and the steep slopes of the park provided great scope for a testing range of obstacles.

This was the year in which Mary Gordon Watson – seen in action across country above – came into her own. The great Cornishman V, originally her father Brigadier Michael Gordon Watson's hunter, had won an Olympic team gold medal with Richard Meade in Mexico the year before, but this year she rode the horse again herself. At Haras du Pin, in Normandy she and Mark Phillips (on Great Ovation) were entered as individuals.

Left: Mary and Mark walking the show jumping course with Dick Stillwell on the last day.

The British team won the gold medal by more than 100 points from the USSR, with West Germany even further behind to take the bronze from France. *Above*: Victory parade for the team (*left to right*) Major Derek Allhusen and Lochinvar, Richard Walker and Pasha (on whom Richard, aged 18, had been Badminton's youngest winner earlier that year), Polyann Hely-Hutchinson on Count Jasper and Staff Sergeant Ben Jones on The Poacher. Mary Gordon Watson and Cornishman (*right*) won the first individual gold medal of their international career – by just over five points from Richard Walker.

Efficiently run by Barry and Jane Wookey at their Vale of Pewsey home, Rushall was the first – probably the only – event to lay telephone lines to each fence to speed the scoring. It was also proud of providing eventing's first flushing loos.

Rushall Horse Trials

Miss Sivewright and Ripalong dominate

By *ALAN SMITH*

PAMELA SIVEWRIGHT and Ripalong, formerly in the British Junior international three-day event team, scored a convincing victory in section four of the inaugural Rushall, Wilts, novice trials yesterday.

Dressage has always been this combination's strongpoint and their test yesterday, for just 15 penalties, was far in front of the others in any of the four sections.

Without jumping faults, either in the ring or across country, they added just 13 for cross-country time to notch an unbeatable 28.

Above left: Malcolm Wallace tackles the 'Avon Flyover' in one of the least elegant moments of his otherwise blameless career. *Left*: The Midland 'M' fence - entered, unsuccessfully, for the sponsors' 'best designed' prize.

For 27 years, over the Easter holiday, Diana Helmore and her mother Mrs Dodo Maxwell, ran an event at Fermyn Woods Hall, their home in Northamptonshire. 1998 would have been the last, but was cancelled because the park was waterlogged.

A former competitor herself, Diana became involved in organisation while working for Lord and Lady Hugh Russell at Wylye. Though severely injured in a road accident in 1980, she continued to play an active part at Brigstock

Right: Diana with Henry Nicoll and course-builder Frank Lurkin.

The team shortlisted to represent Britain in the second World Championships, seen here while in training at the Hindleys' Ribblesdale Park, Ascot. *Left to right:* Mark Phillips (Chicago III), Bridget Parker (Cornish Gold), European Champion Mary Gordon Watson (Cornishman) and Richard Meade (The Poacher). As Cornish Gold was unable to compete, Bridget Parker's place in the team was taken by Stuart Stevens on Benson.

Opposite, below: The grooms for the six shortlisted horses were (*left to right*) Caroline Durston-Smith, Pat Sutton, Julie Buxton, Pippa Tomlin, Jill Dudley and Nicola Norman.

A tough competition was won by Mary Gordon Watson and Cornishman. (*Right*). More than 60 marks behind were Richard Meade and The Poacher. Jimmy Wofford from the USA was a close third on Kilkenny.

Below: The triumphant British team, who won the championship by more than 400 marks from France, the only other nation to complete the team competition: Richard Meade, Mark Phillips, Stuart Stevens and Mary Gordon Watson.

Riding as an individual competitor at her first international championship, Princess Anne *(opposite, above)* won the gold medal on the Queen's home-bred Doublet, having led throughout the competition. Sadly, within the year the horse broke a leg while schooling on the flat in Windsor Great Park and was put down.

Richard Walker *(below, second from left)* was originally selected for the team, but unfortunately his horse Upper Strata went lame and the pair were replaced by Debbie West and Baccarat who contributed to the team gold medal and won the individual silver. In the presentation line-up *(opposite, below)* they are seen with Richard Meade on The Poacher, Captain Mark Phillips on Great Ovation, Mary Gordon Watson on Cornishman V, and chef d'équipe, Colonel Bill Lithgow. Another British individual pair, Stuart Stevens and Classic Chips, won the bronze medal.

Left: Dick Stillwell, highly respected show jumping trainer for many years to this and many other British teams.

This was the first of a run of three team golds (out of a total of 14 to date) for Britain's juniors. *Below*: Chef d'équipe Isobel Reid receives the trophy on behalf of (*l to r*) Amanda Sivewright (Gameel), Andrew Brake (Say When), Christopher Brooke (Olive Oyl) and Lucinda Prior-Palmer (Be Fair).

Christopher Brooke (*right*) won the individual championship on the brilliant dun gelding Olive Oyl – who was barely 15hh – bought by Christopher's father, Lord Brookeborough. We never take ponies', declared Junior selection chairman Colonel 'Babe' Moseley – until Olive Oyl and Christopher won the Junior trial at Tidworth.

Countess Bathurst with 15-year-old Princess Caroline of Monaco at the Midland Bank Championships, Open and Novice, held in Earl Bathurst's Cirencester Park.

1972 | Llanfechain

For many years one of the few two-day events (dressage and show jumping one day, speed and endurance the next), Llanfechain is run by Major Edward Bonnor-Maurice at Bodynfoel Hall, his home in the verdant hill-country of Powys in mid-Wales. The course is a galloping one, on good going, with the Afon Cain featuring in several water jumps.

The European Junior Championships returned to Eridge, where they originated in 1967. This time there were eight teams taking part and Britain won the team championship.

Below, left to right: Pony Club standard bearer in front of chef d'équipe Isobel Reid with, Tony Hill, Christopher Brooke, Alex Colquhoun and Amanda Sivewright. Tony Hill (*left*, on Maid Marion) won the individual silver medal.

The British won team gold by 85 points from the USA, and Richard Meade on Derek Allhusen's Laurieston *(opposite page)*, won the individual gold. Last to set off in a thrilling finish, Richard was told by chef d'équipe Bill Lithgow 'go fast and go clear'. And he did.

Debbie West *(above second from left)* was selected, but Baccarat was lame at the last minute and Bridget Parker *(right, with Mark Phillips, Mary Gordon Watson and Richard Meade)* was chosen to take her place.

A real 'competitors' event, run by the former eventers Toby and Gail Sturgis (left, with sponsor Norman Hills) on their family land in Wiltshire, popular for many years as a pre-Burghley warm-up. The country is flat but two deep river-crossings are a focus for spectators. The year in which Andrew Lloyd Webber (centre, left) came to watch his fiancée Madeleine Gurdon compete, he threw a party for the cast of 'Cats' in the event's marquee.

The customary fine weather enabled time-keepers (above) to work out in the open. Luckily it was fine the year when the hired bus lost its roof under a low bridge on the way to the event and the cross-country control team (left, under the direction of Toby Sturgis) also had to work out in the open. Since 1996 Dauntsey has run as a spring instead of summer event.

The British victory at Pompadour – by nearly 100 marks from silver medalists Germany – also saw the rise of a new star in Virginia Holgate, who was to become Britain's most successful international three day-eventer. One of the team having been withdrawn earlier, Ginny with Dubonnet (*left*), last of the team to start, had to get safely round. She nearly fell off at the first fence, but after that all went well and her clear show jumping just clinched the gold ahead of Sara Bailey riding Red Amber. *Below (l to r)*: Individual riders Melinda Brooke (Olive Oyl) and Dawn Brand (Just a Cloud) with team, Annabel Scrimgeour (Lysander II), Virginia Holgate, Sara Bailey and Geraldine Wilson (Pressos).

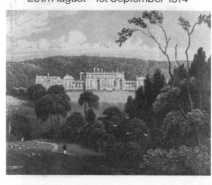

Bramham Horse Trials

29th August – 1st September 1974

H aving begun as a one-
day horse trial, in 1974
Bramham developed into a
three-day event which is
now a major three-star
fixture in the international calendar, directed by Bill
Henson, and includes the
National Young Rider
Championships.
Opposite page: Aerial
view taken in the early
days. *Far left:* Programme
cover for the first event.
Left: Host and organiser,
George Lane-Fox, who has
steadfastly persisted in carrying on with the event during summer weather that has
brought extremes of heat,
humidity, rain and mud, and
has never cancelled.

Top: The horse inspection
takes place in front of the
house. *Above:* View of the
cross-country course, which
makes its way up steep hills
and through woodland.

On the return of the World Championships to Burghley, British hopes were high when Mark Phillips finished the cross-country in the lead. Optimism was shortlived, however, as his horse, the Queen's Columbus, slipped a hock tendon and had to be withdrawn. The US team *(below, left to right)* Mike Plumb on Good Mixture, Denny Emerson (Victor Dakin), Don Sachey (Plain Sailing) and Bruce Davidson (Irish Cap), silver medallists at Munich two years earlier, forged ahead to win the team championship by 270 marks from Great Britain. Davidson (seen on his prize bicycle from sponsors Raleigh) won the individual gold medal, Plumb the silver and Britain's Hugh Thomas, riding Playamar, the bronze.

Left: The late Neil Ayer, tireless leader of eventing in the U.S.A., organiser and international course-designer.
Opposite,below: A fence at Sheila Willcox's Stanton event, where the Americans warmed up for the championships on arrival in this country.

Six girls were selected to defend Britain's Junior team championship title. The horses travelled out by road, surviving the long journey remarkably well. Pratoni was very dusty, but the facilities were first-class. There were no hotels nearby, so parents and supporters set up a British camp (*below*) in one of the few shady places – where riders Annabel Scrimgeour and Diana Clapham were snapped cooling their feet in a bucket of water. There was to be no medal for the team, but Sheila Ker *(left)* riding Lorna Sutherland's Peer Gynt won an individual gold, while team member Joanna Winter took the bronze on Stainless Steel.

By the third day the team was down to three members: Lucinda Prior-Palmer on Be Fair, Princess Anne on Goodwill and Sue Hatherly on Harley – Janet Hodgson's Larkspur having had to be withdrawn from the final inspection after falling twice on the cross-country. Despite a fall in the show jumping for Sue Hatherly, the team finished a good second to the USSR, who had all jumped clear. Lucinda *(left)* won the individual gold medal and Princess Anne the silver. Pietr Gomuschko from the USSR, on Gusar, won the individual bronze and West Germany the team bronze. *Below:* Britain's three lady riders line up for the prize-giving with their chef d'équipe, Lt-Colonel Bill Lithgow.

Firle Place, Sussex home of the Gage family since the 14th century, hosted a run of successful Pony Club area trials until Major Sir Walter Scott, Bt, founded official BHS horse trials here, with the help of members of the Southdown Hunt. *Left:* Course-builder on duty, Sir Walter ('the Major') with regulation equipment – terrier, flagon of cider and battered truck, as described by Debbie Melville *(above)*, former Pony Club competitor at Firle and now organiser.

The Annual Midland Bank Open
and Novice Championships,
after changing venues every two
years, finally came to rest at Locko
Park near Derby, home of the late
Captain Patrick Drury-Lowe *(top
right)*, with its great scope for a
varied cross-country course and excellent viewing for spectators. Joanna
Boswell and Pooch Spiller were regular scorers there, and the event
boasted England's only mounted St John
Ambulance detachment.

The parkland of the Earl of Pembroke's Wilton House, near Salisbury, makes a lovely setting for the cross-country course at this summer fixture. Horses are stabled a mile away at Salisbury Racecourse. The crossing of the River Nadder by the ornate Palladian Bridge, which links the gardens to the park, used to be a spectacular obstacle – until the year when a horse, on descending the two steps into the river, sank too deeply into the water. Regretfully, the organisers decided that a natural river bed was too unstable a base for a competition obstacle.

At Lage-Siekkrug in Germany, Britain won the team championship for the fifth time, after a three-year gap. *Below:* Waiting for the presentation after their clear show jumping round had brought them a 20-point victory over France: Sarah Bouet on Sea Lord V, Caroline Saunders on Cymbal, Fraser Jack on Burnt Oak and Debbie Saffell on Double Brandy. *Right:* Debbie Saffell and Double Brandy, who won the individual silver medal. The bronze went to Sarah Bouet and Sea Lord V.

1976 | Portman

This event in the Portman Hunt country was started in 1976 by John and Susie Woodhouse, seen on the left with their BHS Steward Lord Courtenay. *Below:* Over twenty years later Mrs Woodhouse, who still organises the event, is seen stocking up provisions for her officials. Entering into the spirit of the occasion is tenant farmer John Hosford, over much of whose land the course runs, seen sitting astride the Badger Barrels, named after beer produced by the family firm of Hall & Woodhouse.

Burgie celebrated its 21st birthday in 1998, having grown from novice beginnings to a full-blown, two-star, three-day event. The varied programme is run by Hamish and Pollyann Lochore at their home, an Equestrian Centre near Forres, where the steep slopes of the cross-country give excellent viewing for spectators – plus a splendid outlook over the Moray Firth.

Horses assemble in a paddock in front of the house before trotting up for inspection by the Ground Jury from the front steps. Beyond this, another paddock provides a beautiful setting for the dressage. Competitors drive hundreds of miles from all over the British Isles to enjoy the fun and informality of this event.

This was a momentous event for Lucinda Prior-Palmer, as she became the first rider to defend her European title successfully *(opposite page)* She also contributed to the British team gold medal with *(above)* Clarissa Strachan on Merry Sovereign, Jane Holderness-Roddam (Warrior) and Christopher Collins (Smokey VI).

During the Championships Lucinda was feeling beset with problems, her strength and spirits at a low ebb following the death of her beloved father. Her horse, Mrs Elaine Straker's George – on whom Lucinda had won Badminton that spring – seemed equally lethargic. On the steeplechase Lucinda fell off and was dragged along, but outside the fence penalty zone, and, having remounted, she still finished inside the time.

She has described one memorable episode on the unhappy cross-country ride: 'I think I would have cried and flopped off then and there, I felt so weak, but for an English country gentleman, who raised his shooting stick high in the air as George, head low and heavy, mouth dead, galloped by, and shouted "Come on England, come on George".'

Blair Castle (78 -)
Burgie (78 -)
Chepstow (78 -)
Chessington (78, 79)
Clandon Park (78 - 82)
Crondall (78 - 87)
Dalmahoy (78 - 88)
Frome (78 - 91)
Gleddoch (78 - 86)
Hampton on the Hill (78 - 89)
Harlton (78 - 87)
Murton (78 - 82)
Northampton (78 -)
Tythrop (78 -)
Wensleydale (78 - 80)

Braintree (79 - 85)
Cardigan (79 - 80)
Heckfield (79 - 88)
Iping (79 -)
Markyate (79 -)
Shelswell (79 - 82)
Shipley Park (79 - 82)
Stowell Park (79 - 85)
Stratford upon Avon (79 - 85)
Swaffham (79 - 85)
Waldridge Manor (79 - 88)

Abergavenny (80, 81)
Aldon (80 -)
Belton Park (80 -)
Boville Park (80 - 82)
Brockenhurst (80 - 82, 85 -)
Carluke (80)
Codford St Mary (80 - 86)
Denbigh (80 - 83)
Lyme Park (80 - 93)
Pebworth Vale (80 - 89)
Ragley Hall (80 -)
Rotherfield (80 - 91)
Springhill (80 -)
Tenby (80 - 92)
Wintershall (80 - 85)

Auchterarder (81, 82)
Castle Howard (81-84)
Clumber Park (81 -)
Hagley Hall (81 - 87)
Holdenby (81 -)
Holker Hall (81 - 92)
Marsden Manor (81 - 91)
Smith's Lawn (81 -)
Wynyard Park (81 - 88)

Burton Constable (82)
Congleton (82, 83)
Downton Castle (81 - 89)
Killerton (82 -)
Oulton Park (82 - 86)

Thirlestane Castle (82 -)

Albourne (83 - 90)
Berriewood (83 -)
Bourton (83 - 88)
Castle Ashby (83 - 85)
Chelsworth Park (83 -)
Copt Oak (83 - 92)
Ellon (83 - 92)
Gatcombe Park (83 -)
Hogshaw (83 - 90)
Church Crookham (88 - 90)
Croxton Park (88 - 90)
Downfield (89)
Goring Heath (89 -)
Highclere (88 -)
Longworth (83 - 91, 94, 95)
Mayfield (83)
Newbury (83 - 97)
Peper Harow (83 -)
Ripley Castle (83 - 91)
Rowallan Castle (83 - 92)
Shamley Green (83 - 96)
Stowe (83 - 94)
Urchinwood Manor (83 -)
Uttoxeter (83)
Windsor Forest Stud (83 - 85)
Witton Castle (83 -)

Auchinleck (84 -)
Bathampton (84)
Brendon Hill (84 -)
Henbury Hall (84 -)
Lulworth Castle (84 -)
Poplar Park (84 -)
Rogate (84, 85)
Wokingham (84 -)

Dynes Hall (85 -)
Hilton Park (85 -
King's Somborne (85 - 92)
Lincolnshire (85 -)
Shawdene (85 - 87)
York (85 - 90)

Barnsley Park (86 - 92)
Brightling Park (86 -)
Dodington Park (86 - 93)
Glenluce (86 - 95)
Hopton Court (86 -)
Jervaulx (86 - 96)
Lanhydrock (86 -)
Lowesby (86 -)
Montacute (86 -)
Pembrey Park (86 -)
Stilemans (86 -)
Withcote Hall (86 -)

Barthorpe (87 - 91)

Brockwood (87 -)

Crews Hill (87 - 90)
Culzean (87 -)
Drummond Castle (87 - 89)
Larkhill (87 -)
Logie (87 - 89)
Longleat (87 -)
Mortonhall (87 - 92)
Offchurch Bury (87 - 92)
Powderham (87 -)
Wolterton Hall (87 - 90)

Running any kind of event, whether one-, two- or three-day, is a demanding, time-consuming and sometimes thankless business. However, this does not seem to have deterred people up and down the land from taking on the onerous role of organiser or providing help in many different ways, for by the end of the '70s the fixture list had grown to 150 events covering all parts of the country, located in a variety of delightful settings from stately homes to small farms and supported by an army of enthusiastic and energetic volunteers.

In addition to the overall benefit of Midland Bank's support, many of the leading riders were by this time securing their own sponsorship, which enabled them to maintain a string of horses coming up through the grades.

When the Bank finally withdrew from the scene in 1985 a new generation of corporate sponsors emerged, which helped to keep the momentum going. Private ownership also began to have its attractions, and played an increasingly important part in the production of team horses.

In the summer of 1978 a cataclysmic event took place in the delightful bluegrass country of Lexington, Kentucky – at the World Championships, in which unforeseen heat, humidity and airlessness had a devastating effect on the horses. The Canadians, who were under orders to get safely round the cross-country without pressing for speed, won the team gold medal and Bruce Davidson (USA) the individual gold. At the end of the speed and endurance Bruce's young horse Might Tango required drastic treatment for heat exhaustion and was never able to repeat his brilliance. The British failed to finish as a team, but Richard Meade was fifth on Bleak Hills and Jane Starkey, riding as an individual on her plucky Topper Too, finished seventh to salvage some national pride.

The 1980 Olympics brought further frustration when the decision was taken not to send a team to Moscow, in protest against the Russian invasion of Afghanistan. In the 'Alternative Olympics' at Fontainebleau, rated as a World Championship, the British team again failed to complete.

In 1980, Gill Watson was appointed trainer to the Juniors, and in 1981- the year in which Mark Phillips won his fourth Badminton to the Young Riders too, when their championships were inaugurated at Achselschwang. A highly successful policy of nurturing the young had already been established in the late '60s and early '70s by Colonel Babe Moseley, followed by Colonel Hubert Allfrey, Colonel Bill Lithgow and then Viscount Allenby. Under the outstanding 16-year leadership of young Riders chairman Christopher Schofield, succeeded by David Merrett, Gill embarked on what was to be an unsurpassed run of success.

Towards the end of the '80s the Pony riders – led first by Mrs Jane Whiteley and then by Mrs Jane Rook, and trained by Gill's assistant Juliet Snelson, succeeded by former Young Rider medallist Jonquil Hemming – were formally recognised as an official international team. Another highly successful innovation during this decade was the founding in 1978 of the Horse Trials Support Group by Martin Whiteley (its first Chairman), Christopher Collins, Tim Holderness-Roddam and Tom Greenhalgh, with Jane Pontifex as Hon Secretary. Its aim was to enlist private subscribers who wished to support the training and development of talented riders for British teams. Some 200 members were enrolled and the organisation has continued to flourish, giving an annual scholarship and funding training courses each year for promising riders in all team categories. Added to this have been the tireless fund-raising efforts of committee member Mrs Rosemary Barlow.

The decade was also notable for the continuing ascendancy of lady riders, which had begun with Lucinda Prior-Palmer in the mid-'70s and continued with her and Virginia Holgate into the late '80s. Lucinda's six Badminton wins and Ginny's four consecutive Burghley titles are unlikely to be equalled. Also during the 1980s, regional officers were appointed to help with the growing administration of the sport.

In 1984 Colonel Peter Hodgson retired, to be succeeded as Director of Horse Trials by Major Tim Taylor. Soon after this, the sport suffered a severe blow in the sudden death of Martin Whiteley, Chairman of the Horse Trials Committee. Laurence Rook temporarily returned to the chairmanship until the election of Hugh Neil. In 1986 Charles Stratton, who had directed Burghley for eight years, was succeeded by Bill Henson.

In 1987 a new system of balloting helped to provide a fairer chance of running horses at over-subscribed events – an increasing problem, especially with the not-infrequent cancellation of spring events due to bad weather: which happened at Badminton that same year.

The white battlements of Blair Castle are a striking sight beside the main route through the Central Highlands. Founded in the 13th century, it is the ancestral home of the Earls, and now Dukes, of Atholl. The late 10th Duke bred Highland ponies here and was a keen supporter of the annual horse trials.

After 12 years the event graduated from a one-day to a three-day, and in 1996 staged the Junior European Championships.

Scotland's leading course-designer Ronald Alexander, a professional architect and former horse trials competitor and organiser, is responsible for the course, which ranges from the flat parkland of the valley to the steep slopes above the castle, commanding lovely views.

The trials have had a number of directors over the years but the organisation has always been based on the office of the Factor, Andrew Gordon.

On one of the evenings during the event all competitors and officials are invited to a splendid Scottish gathering, at which kilts or tartan trews are *de rigueur* for those who are entitled to wear them.

Over the four days of the event there are many other activities which attract competitors and spectators alike: show jumping, Pony Club Games, Highland ponies and cattle, and a full programme of displays and contests in the Highland Country Fair.

Sitting on the fence (left to right) Flavia Clarke with Jenny McGregor and Diana Bown, former and present organisers of the two-day event held on Chepstow racecourse. *Below:* Scorer at work in the caravan.

Above: Cross-country control centre. *Right:* Programme cover-drawing of Piercefield Park, focal point of the event.

Under the direction first of Kit Dwerryhouse and later of Mrs Janet Plant, the Earl of Bradford's Weston Park, in Shropshire, became a major horse trials venue, running one-and two-day events at all levels as well as the annual Pony Club Championships.

Prim Palmer was a popular figure at this and many other events, distributing competitors' number-cloths, while her husband Noel – seen below briefing fence judges – was one of the HTG's technical advisers and course-designers.

This was the year in which Windsor expanded from a one- and two-day event to a full-scale three-day event, which now includes the National Junior Championships. The Princess Royal, President, and the Queen, Patron, are seen talking to Colonel Frank Beale, Vice-President, with committee members and officials. Sally Merrick, on the left, is still entries secretary.

Below: Mrs Peggy Maxwell, Director, is knocked down while trying to shield the Princess from a prize-winner's horse.

Opposite page: Mrs Maxwell and Colonel Beale with Bill Thomson, technical adviser. Like father like son: Captain Mark Phillips on the roads and tracks and Peter Phillips, a mounted Pony Club runner, collecting jump judges' scoresheets.

The Copper Horse is a spectacular viewing point for both the Great Park and the cross-country course.

Loyal subject saves Anne from horse

LONDON: A woman flung herself in front of a bolting horse to save Princess Anne from being trampled, it was revealed yesterday.

The princess was presenting trophies at the Windsor Horse Trials when a frightened horse reared out of control and stampeded towards her.

The show's director, 60-year-old Peggy Maxwell, threw herself in front of the princess and crashed to the ground, scattering her tray of ribbons.

Both were unhurt and Mrs Maxwell managed a wan smile as Anne helped her to her feet.

"It was reflex action," said Mrs Maxwell later.

1979 | Iping

Iping is a summer event held in the grounds of Hammerwood, home of Mr Michael Lakin and his wife, The Honourable Mrs Lakin, who ran the event until she retired in 1998. The photographs span her 21 years as organiser: *Left*: Mrs (Daphne) Lakin, on right, in the early days of the event with Colin Wares, Sue Tucker and Phillipa Magill. *Below left*: In 1998, with Ann Inskip, who was cross-country steward for the first 17 years until moving from the area, and returns every year to lend her support.

Below: The water jump has always been one of the main features of the hilly cross-country course which winds its way over adjoining land owned by Mrs Forshall and Mr Tim Coyte, in a delightful West Sussex setting.

Nicola May (inset), second of the four daughters of England cricket captain Peter May and his eventing wife Virginia, won the individual gold medal with Commodore IV, the family's stalwart chestnut *(above)*. She finished on her dressage score, well clear of the other competitors, who battled it out for the silver and bronze medals. The British team of Sarah Calloway, Tuffy Tilley, Brigit Ensten and Nicola came second in a close contest for the team medals.

123

The steep-sided valley of the park at Aldon, near Yeovil, Somerset, the property of Mr and Mrs Henry Batten, is an ideal setting for this spring event, organised by Mrs Batten.

The Junior European Championships of 1980 were held at Achselschwang, in Bavaria, which has since become venue of an international three-day event. *Below:* The gold medal winnig British team, Virginia Strawson (Greek Herb), Susanna Brooke (Super Star IV), Nicola May (Commodore IV) and Claire Needham (Solo), with their chef d'équipe Mrs Isobel Reid. *Left:* In a close finish for the individual medals Claire Needham and Solo won the silver.

The first European Young Rider Championships were staged by Germany, also at Achselschwang. *Above:* The British gold-medal-winning team with their chef d'équipe James Mackie: Maureen Piggott on Asian Princess, Sheena Trewitt (Unusual), Lucy Bywater (Countryman) and Beverley Thomas (Divine Intervention).

In the '90s Lucy Bywater *(left and above)*, now Lucy Thompson, achieved fame riding for Ireland. At Pratoni in 1995 she won the Open European Championships on Welton Romance.

The British team's well-judged and efficient performance at Horsens in Denmark brought them the team championship, under the leadership of chef d'équipe Malcom Wallace. In the picture above he is seen with the team and their grooms (all wearing spotted bandanas) at the training centre before leaving for Denmark. Riders and horses (from left to right) were Elizabeth Purbrick and Peter the Great, Virginia Holgate and Priceless (6th), Diana Clapham (individual) and Windjammer II, Richard Meade and Kilcashel (7th), Sue Benson and Gemma Jay, and Rachel Bayliss (individual) with Mystic Minstrel. Apart from the French, who finished 6th, the British were the only team to go clear in the show jumping (with just a 0.25 time penalty for Sue Benson.)

127

Luhmühlen, which lies on historic Luneberg Heath, is Germany's oldest established three-day event, and has staged many international competitions. Its first European Championship in 1975 was won by Lucinda Prior-Palmer on Be Fair. In 1982, now Lucinda Green, she returned to win the World

Championship on Australian-bred Regal Realm (*opposite*). Though dressage was not Regal Realm's strongest phase, he was the only horse to incur no further penalties.

Britain also won the team gold medal (*above*) in a close fight with West Germany. 'The thoroughly competent performance of both team

and individual riders at all stages of the battle', reported Colonel Frank Weldon in *Horse and Hound*, 'made their many supporters feel proud to be British... but they had to work hard for their honour'.

Virginia Holgate started first for Britain, on Priceless – and ended up in seventh

place. Rachel Bayliss, leader in the dressage on Mystic Minstrel, came next, but a missed foothold at the first water complex incurred 20 penalties and they finished 22nd. Both Lucinda and Richard Meade (fourth rider for Britain on Kilcashel) were required to produce a clear round within the time, and both delivered. It was nip and tuck for the final show jumping, but only Meade had a fence down so victory was theirs. Individuals Clarissa Strachan on Merry Sovereign and Diana Clapham on (Windjammer) finished 6th and 10th respectively.

The championships were marred by the tragic death of a Swiss rider, Ernst Baumann, substitute for the horse's usual rider: which may have led to a moment's uncertainty when taking off in the final water complex towards the end of the course. The horse hit the fence above his knees, the rider was thrown over the fence, and the horse fell on top of him.

At Rotherfield Park the British Juniors won both gold medals, ahead of the Poles, the French and three other nations. *Left:* Isobel Reid (chef d'équipe) with l to r: Katherine Gracey on Rustic Rambler, Anne Marie Taylor on Gin and Orange, Ros Bevan on Horton Venture and Karen Straker on Running Bear.

A clear show jumping round from Karen Straker (*below left*) won her the individual gold medal when the current leader had two fences down.

Above: At Fontainebleau in the Young Rider Championships Virginia Strawson and Minsmore led from start to finish to win the individual gold medal.

Watching the team take the silver in a close finish were *(from left)* Shrimp and Jamie Mackie, Christopher and Angela Schofield, Colonel Hubert Allfrey, Henry and Joan Nicoll, Jane Pontifex and Bob Baskerville.

The ancestral home of the Maitlands is the setting for the annual Scottish Horse Trials Championships. Host and president is The Honorable Gerald ('Bunny') Maitland-Carew, seen with his sister Baroness Diana Wrangel, and elder brother Patrick, Lord Carew. As children they used to bring their ponies from Ireland to compete in the Pony Club Championships, staying with their grandmother, the Countess of Lauderdale, at Thirlestane Castle (which she left to Bunny).

131

Britain's Juniors successfully defended the team and individual championships that they had won at Rotherfield Park the previous year. Helen Brown *(left)* in her one international appearance took the individual gold on Mrs Louise King's Fleetwater Opposition. The British team also won gold *(below, left to right):* Susanna Macaire on Latin Tempo, Helen Brown, Rachel Hunt on Friday Fox and Sarah Williams on Spiritos. Both Susanna and Rachel went on to ride for Britain in Young Rider and senior teams.

The site at Pratoni was by now very different from its uncultivated state during the 1960 Olympic Games and was established as a national training centre for Italy's three day eventers. Since Roman times, the area, in unspoiled countryside near some famous beauty spots, has attracted equestrian activities. Today it provides a magnificent setting for one of the world's finest cross-country courses: ideal for spectators with its high-up views and exciting water jumps. The Italian Pony Club is also very active in this area.

The British team *(top)* of Karen Straker on Running Bear, Polly Schwerdt (Dylan II), Camilla Murdoch (Rugan) and Virginia Strawson (Minsmore) regained the gold medal in a runaway victory from France. Karen *(right)* won individual silver, little more than one point behind France's Jean-Paul Saint Vignes, and Polly won the bronze.

In the line-up above they are joined by chef d'équipe James Mackie, Chairman Christopher Schofield, trainer Gill Watson and vet Bob Baskerville.

Peter Scott-Dunn, for 31 years official vet to the British team, travelled many thousands of miles to international events all over the world, using his skill and experience to keep horses fit and sound, especially for the crucial inspection on the last day. With him (*above*) is his wife Ann, an expert in faradism, who also became a valued member of the team.

Rachel Bayliss and Mystic Minstrel, gold medallists, *top left*; and centre with Lucinda Green and Regal Realm (silver). Rachel's score as an individual did not count towards the team total, so Britain won silver behind Sweden. *Right:* Rachel with team members Lorna Clarke, Lucinda Green and Ginny Holgate. The fourth team member was Diana Clapham.

The Princess Royal's home in the Cotswolds forms a dramatic setting for the National Open Championships, and Mark Phillips makes full use of its natural features in designing a challenging course. The cross-country is run in reverse order of placing, so that the excitement of the competition builds up right to the end of the day, when the Princess presents the prizes.

Lucinda Green's record in winning Badminton six time, on six different horses, is unlikely ever to be equalled, let alone beaten. In 1973 *(top left)* it was with her own Be Fair, European champion in 1975. In 1976: *(top right)* with Mrs Vicki Phillips's Wide Awake who tragically collapsed and died during his lap of honour. In 1977 *(centre left)* with Mrs Elaine Straker's George, European Champion the same year. In 1979 *(centre right)*

Charles Cyzer's Killaire. In 1983 *(above)* SR Direct Mail's Regal Realm, who had been World Champion in 1982. In 1984 *(right)*: SR Direct Mail's Beagle Bay.

Lucinda Green (*previous page*) had the honour of carrying the Union Jack at the head of the British Olympic contingent at the opening ceremony.
Left: Gold medal winners: Mark Todd (New Zealand) riding Charisma. A bronze medal for Virginia Holgate (*below*) and silver for the British team, Virginia Holgate, Ian Stark, Diana Clapham and Lucinda Green. *Below left*, The British team in Windjammer's box during training, with shortlisted rider Robert Lemieux. *Opposite*: Medal ceremony, and celebration with chef d'équipe Malcolm Wallace.

Britain won the team gold medal, as well as individual silver for Philippa Magill (riding as an individual) and bronze for Rachel Hunt.

Below The riders with Rachel's Friday Fox, *left to right*: Virginia Strawson (the other individual), Rachel Hunt, Mandy Orchard, Philippa Magill, Polly Schwerdt, Jonquil Sainsbury.

Above, with the Young Rider Committee (left to right) Lady Doreen (Bunty) Prior-Palmer, chef d' équipe Jamie Mackie, Christopher Schofield (chairman and chief mentor for 16 years), trainer Gill Watson, Colonel Henry Nicoll and Lt-Colonel Bill Lithgow.

The first Midland Bank Novice Championship, held at Chatsworth, was won by Sarah Roger-Smith riding Gambit *(top left)*. The Open Championship began in 1970 and from then until their final running in 1985 both championships were held at Wylye *(above)*, Cirencester Park *(left)*, Goodwood *(bottom left)* and finally at Locko Park *(below)*.

141

The British team won their third successive gold medal at the championships held for the first time at Le Lion d'Angers – which then became an annual CCI. They were (left to right) Anne Marie Taylor on Justyn Thyme VI, Ros Bevan on Horton Venture, Claire Oseman on Another Fred and Rachel Hunt on Friday Fox.

In a close finish for the individual medals, Claire Oseman (*left*) completed with only her dressage penalties to win the gold when West Germany's Peter Kruemmel hit a show jump.

143

This year Britain was able to field a first-class team of highly experienced riders on well-proven horses and at Burghley they vanquished the opposition to win the team championship by 181 points, as well as all three individual medals.

Below Something to smile about: Lorna Clarke, who won the silver (seen also on right with Myross, jumping into the Trout Hatchery); Virginia Holgate, gold; and Ian Stark, bronze. The other team member, Lucinda Green, was 6th on Regal Realm – always a brilliant jumper but not so impressive in the dressage arena. Of the six additional individual riders entered by Britain as host nation, Mandy Orchard was 4th on Venture Busby and Clarissa Strachan 10th on Delphy Dazzle.

Ginny Holgate – who had beaten Mark Todd to win at Badminton in the spring – rode her usual exemplary dressage test on Priceless (*left*), just five marks behind the leader, and incurred no further penalties throughout the championship. She was the only competitor to achieve this.

Below: Proud moment for the team and their chef d' équipe Lord Patrick Beresford as they stand to attention for the national anthem before the presentation of medals. *From left to right*, Lorna Clarke and Myross, Ian Stark and Oxford Blue, Virginia Leng and Priceless, Lucinda Green and Regal Realm.

P rincess Anne presents gold medals to Alexandra Ramus on Spy Story, Steven Chambers on Talisman SC, Clea Hoeg on Norton Bay and Sally Bateson on Scalphunter, watched by happy grooms (*below*). *Left*: Georgina Anstee and Printer's Devil, who won the individual bronze.

This year the British team won all the medals. *Left*: Briefing by chef d' équipe Jamie Mackie and team vet Bob Baskerville. *Centre, and bottom left*: Gold medal winners Alexandra Ramus and Spy Story II, who were competing as individuals. *Bottom right*: The winning team: Julie-Anne Shield on Crimdon Lucky George, Judith Copland on Sweeny, Vanessa Ashbourne on Hector James (individual silver medal winners), Rachel Hunt on Friday Fox (bronze medal).

Montacute House, an Elizabethan mansion dating back to 1580, near Yeovil in Somerset, was one of the first properties to be acquired by the National Trust. From 1986 until 1995 the horse trials, originally introduced as a successor to Sherborne, were run by Mary and Larry Moore; they are now organised by Mike Felton, Master of the Blackmore and Sparkford Vale Hunt. *Above*: Front-of-house spectacular. *Left* Backstage Workers: a scene typical of events throughout the country.

Above: Larry Moore builds a fence which is to be called 'The Dog Kennels.' *Right*: He points out the place where it will be sited. *Below left*: It ends up, for sponsors, as 'The Tea Chests'. *Below right*: Mary Moore presents Mark Todd with the solid silver Daily Telegraph Cup, inherited from Sherborne. It was originally donated at the request of Captain Lionel Dawson RN, the Daily Telegraph's equestrian correspondent, who hunted with the Blackmore and Sparkford Vale.

These were the first international championships to be held in Australia. For the British horses it meant a three-week period of quarantine in Australia on top of the three weeks that they had already spent in quarantine at Wylye.

Eight nations sent teams, and the result was a great victory for the British. New Zealand's Tinks Pottinger was in the lead after the second day but had to withdraw her horse, Volunteer, so Ginny Leng and Priceless (*left,* jumping the brewer's dray) were able to clinch the gold.

Above: The victorious British team (left to right) Lorna Clarke (Myross), Ginny Leng, Ian Stark (Oxford Blue), Clarissa Strachan (Delphy Dazzle). *Right:* Lorna Clarke receives her bronze medal from Prince Philip.

Four months later, the British team were on the road again, this time across Europe to Bialy Bor, where the FEI had authorised Poland to run another team championship as a possible substitute for Gawler. Once again, the British won the team championship, while Virginia Leng, this time on Night Cap (*below*), won the individual gold and Ian Stark on Sir Wattie (*below right*) the silver. *Right*: Ginny, Ian and chef d' équipe Lord Patrick Beresford are joined in the victory parade by Rachel Hunt on Piglet and Madeleine Gurdon on The Done Thing.

Photocall with the Duke of Beaufort for the team during training at Badminton. *Left to right:* Richard Walker, Rachel Hunt, Mark Phillips, Lucinda Green, Virginia Leng, Jane Thelwall, Ian Stark.
Below: The team – Ginny on Night Cap, Ian (Sir Wattie), Rachel (Aloaf) and Lucinda (Shannagh, but riding a borrowed horse for the prize giving) – won the gold medal from West Germany. Shannagh fell at the influential road crossing; then Aloaf pecked badly at the same fence, unseating Rachel, but the horse managed to keep his feet and the rider clung on to get back into the saddle, so they completed the course with only a few time penalties.

Right: Ginny Leng on Night Cap, having scored the best dressage marks of all, went on to complete both the cross-country and the show jumping without further penalties and to win her fourth successive individual gold medal. *Below*: A pause while walking the course for (*left to right*) Bunty Prior-Palmer, Ginny's trainer Dot Willis, Lucinda, Mark (*standing*), Jane Thelwall (the other individual, with King's Jester) and Ginny.

Left: Ian Stark riding Sir Wattie, on whom he had won Badminton the year before and was to do so again in 1988. Like Ginny and Night Cap, the pair incurred no further penalties to add to their dressage score, and carried off the silver medal. The bronze medal went to Germany's Claus Erhorn riding Justyn Thyme, bought from Anne Marie Taylor, who had ridden the horse into fifth place in the World Championships at Gawler.

There was to be no team medal for the Young Riders on their first visit to Poland, but Pippa Nolan *(left)* made her debut on the international scene to win the individual gold medal, riding her sparky blue roan Sir Barnaby *(below)*.

Right: Photocall for the team (Judith Copland, Ruth House, Susanna Macaire and Katie Parker) with Pippa Nolan who went as an individual, Judith Cope, who dropped out, and Sarah Kellard, who took her place as reserve. With them are team vet Bob Baskerville, trainer Gill Watson and chef d'équipe Giles Rowsell.

Britain's winning team (*left to right*): Kristina Gifford on Song and Dance Man, Polly Lyon (Highland Road), Andrea Morris (Jack O'Lantern) and Claire Bowley (Fair Share).

Above, left: The individual gold medal winners, Polly Lyon and Highland Road, in the arena on the final day, when they jumped a clear round. After the dressage they were one point behind West Germany's Martina Kruemmel on Waldfee, but overtook them with a better cross-country score, as did William Fox-Pitt and Steadfast (*above, right*), who won the silver medal.

Bishop Burton (88 -)
Blenheim (88 -)
Bramcote (88, 89, 92, 93)
Burnham Beeches (88 -)
Inveraray (88 -)
Lockinge (88 - 92)
Monmouth (88 -)
Penton (88 -)
Rickmansworth (88)
Skipton (88 -)
St Andrews (88- 91)
Ston Easton Park (88 -)
Tetton Hall (88 -)
Withybrook (88 - 92)
Wolverhampton (88- 90)

Auchleven (88- 90)
Buckminster Park (89 -)
Callington (88 - 96)
Charney Bassett (88 - 91)
Danny Park (88 - 92)
Dolphinton (88 - 91)
Dunsfold Ryse (88 - 95)
Gleneagles (89 -)
Hanslope (89)
Kincardine O'Neil (89 -)
Langton (88 - 93)
Lyneham (89 - 96)
Nettleton (89 - 92)
Osbaldeston (89 -)
Trefnant (89 - 96)
Wellow Park (89 - 94)
Winmarleigh Hall (89 - 91)

Althorp (90 - 94)
Bradwall (90 -)
Ferney Hall (90 -)
Hexham (90 -)
Isleham (90 -)
Milton Keynes (90 -)
Savernake Forest (90 -)

Ashurst (91 - 96)
Biddlesden Park (91 - 93)
Bold Heath (91 -)
Borough Court (91 -)
Carlisle (91 -)
Garth House (91 - 96)
Great Witchingham (91 - 96)
Hartpury (91 -)
Ivesley (91 -)
Moulton (91 - 95)
Parkgate (91 -)
Uggeshall (91 - 94)

Ashby Puerorum (92 - 95)
Catton Park (92 -)
Cornbury Park (92 -)

Crockstead Park (92 -)
Doddershall Park (92)
Glamis (92 - 94)
Gotham (92 - 94)
Hilmarton (92 - 96)
Lytham Hall (92 - 95)
Moreton Morrell (92 -)
Petworth (92 -)
Stanford Rivers (92 -)

Borde Hill (93 -)
Bretton Park (93 -)
Cleobury Mortimer (93 -)
Gatcombe (93 -)
Hopetoun (93 -)
Oatridge (93 -)
Rodbaston (93 -)

Somerleyton Hall (93 -)
Stockland Lovell (93 -)
Storeton Hall (93 - 96)
Thornton-le-Dale (93 - 95)
Yorkshire (93 -)

Knaptoft (94 -)
Osmaston Park (94 -)
Oving (94 -)
Purston Manor (94 -)
Tutbury (94 -)

Llanover (95 -)
Sansaw (95 -)
Stonar School (95 -)
Winkburn Park (95 -)

Berrington Hall (96 -)
St Michaels (96 -)
Syde (96 -)

Allerton Park (97 -)
Castletown (97 -)
Duchy College (97 -)
Hambleden (97 -)
Houston (97 -)
Lymington (97 -)
Pencoed (97 -)
Somerley Park (97 -)
West Wilts (97 -)
Wilmslow (97 -)

This was undoubtedly the decade of the New Zealanders who, using Britain as their base, dominated competitive eventing. They did it not with theories, or a tight training structure, or cut-and-dried plans, but with natural flair, instinctive horsemanship and a positive attitude. Leading the Kiwi pack was Mark Todd, who in the previous decade had already established himself as head and shoulders above every other event rider, as well as one of the world's finest all-round horseman. Following in his footsteps came Blyth Tait, who during the 1990s notched up the World Championship at Stockholm in 1990; the Olympic title in Atlanta (1996); and the Burghley and World Championships (Rome) in 1998.

Mark Todd's care for his horses was demonstrated by his preparation for the 1988 Seoul Olympics, when he and the 17-year-old Charisma competed in just four one-day events – Belton, where they were 2nd, Brockenhurst (3rd) Holker Hall (unplaced) and the British Open Championships at Gatcombe (1st) – before going on to win their second successive Olympic gold medal ahead of Ian Stark and Ginny Leng.

At home, 1989 brought the end of an era in the death of Colonel Frank Weldon, who was probably the most influential figure in the sport's history. An experienced horseman, and Commanding Officer of the King's Troop RHA, he led British teams to their first international successes. On retirement from the army he was appointed director and course-designer at Badminton, where his skills, sound judgement, administrative ability and sheer force of personality carried the event to worldwide pre-eminence. As chairman of the HTC's rules committee for many years, he also forged the guidelines which now govern the sport internationally.

In 1991 Hugh Neill retired as Chairman of Horse Trials, to which he had brought business acumen as well as efficient administration, and was succeeded by John Tulloch.

The 1992 Olympic Games in Barcelona brought no joy for the British, but underlined the strength of the riders from Australia and New Zealand. However, in 1994 and 1995 Britain overcame all opposition to win gold in the World Equestrian Games at The Hague and the Open European Championships at Pratoni del Vivaro in Italy.

The 1996 Olympic Games at Atlanta brought an innovation in the introduction of separate team and individual competitions, following the IOC's new policy of awarding only one medal for one performance.

Grave doubts had been expressed about running the three-day event during the height of Atlanta's summer heat and humidity, but under instructions from the FEI, intense veterinary research – in which the Animal Health Trust at Newmarket played a big part – ensured that no horse suffered from the adverse conditions.

In 1997 Michael Allen succeeded to the chairmanship of horse trials when John Tulloch was appointed President of the British Equestrian Federation. During this year the Horse Trials Group took the momentus step of breaking away from the British Horse Society to set up as a limited company under the name of The British Horse Trials Association (BHTA). For years it had been felt

that the sport ought to have its own identity and to be in full control of its own finances. Furthermore, the BEF, of which it was part and which was affiliated to the FEI, could not remain indefinitely under the wing of the BHS, a registered charity.

The substantial financial reserves deposited by horse trials over the years had to remain with the BHS but could be drawn upon to fund training schemes – which was within the BHS's charitable remit. Substantial government funding is at last being channelled to the sport through the National Lottery and the Sports Aid Foundation.

This decade was marred by the tragic deaths of two young men killed while competing at three-day events: Mark Davies at Burghley in 1988 and Richard Adams at Windsor in 1993. In memory of her son, Jane Davies founded the Mark Davies Injured Riders Fund, which has given financial help to riders suffering serious injury, while Ann and David Adams provided the Richard Adams Memorial Ambulances for the Royal Berkshire Ambulance Service.

The golden jubilee year has seen a major shake-up of administrative roles, in which Giles Rowsell was appointed Chairman of the British Equestrian Team Committee, responsible under the BEF for the distribution of funds to horse trials. The BEF appointed Dawson Buck as its chief executive and secretary general, an appointment which was to be followed by that of a managing director to the BHTA, responsible for business development, finance and administration, with Tim Taylor continuing as Horse Trials Director, in charge of the running of the national sport.

Whatever goes on behind the scenes, it is riders and horses who matter most, and for them 1998 had its ups and downs – with Christopher Bartle's exciting Badminton win on Word Perfect, his misfortunes and those of other riders leading up to the World Championships at Pratoni, followed by the British team bronze, won against great odds.

The annual conference (now the BHTA AGM) is attended by organisers, and other interested parties, some of whom can be recognised in the photograph above.

The selection committee (*below*) at the Holker Hall final team trial for the Seoul Olympics: (left to right) executive officer Jamie Mackie, Chairman Henrietta Knight, Charles Harrison, Jane Holderness-Roddam, Mary Gordon Watson and Michael Tucker.

B|lenheim is the final three-day event of the autumn, run by Mike Etherington-Smith as a three-star international. *Above:* The Palace makes a magnificent backdrop for the roads and tracks on one side and for the main arena on the other, where the Duke of Marlborough, accompanied by Richard Ide (for first sponsors Audi), is shown presenting prizes to the Irish team *(right):* David Foster, Sally Corscadden, James Coonan and Fiona Wentges, with their chef d'équipe Eric Horgan.

For the riders from six-teen nations who took part, the Olympic Games in Seoul was a speculative venture. South Korea had no experience of running a three-day event – though they had sent riders to train in Britain for several seasons in advance – but Britain's Hugh Thomas had been appointed course-designer and all the official posts requiring technical skill or experience, such as jump judges, were filled by volunteers from other nations with an eventing background.
Above: Mark Todd and Charisma on their way to winning a second Olympic individual gold medal. *Left:* Ian Stark and Sir Wattie, who won the silver.

Ginny Leng *(above)* won the individual bronze medal with Master Craftsman, having survived being jumped right out of the saddle early on the course. *Right:* Gold medallists Mark Todd and Charisma. *Below:* Silver medals for Britain's team (left to right) Ian Stark, Ginny Leng, Karen Straker, and Mark Phillips (who withdrew Cartier after Phase C).

The British won the team gold by the narrowest of margins (1.60) from West Germany. *Left*: Alice Clapham, Sophie Newman and Kristina Gifford. The fourth member of the team, David England (*centre, right*) was absent because of a badly broken arm. *Centre, left*: Bronze medallists Tina Gifford and Smithstown Lad. *Below, left*: Team trainer, Gill Watson, communing with a friend. *Below, right:* Winning smiles from Alice, Tina and Sophie.

At Limburg-Zonhoven in Belgium, Polly Lyon and High-land Road (*above*) won their second gold and also helped the team to victory. *Right:* The champion, with trophy.

Top: The winning team: William Fox-Pitt and Stead-fast, Polly Lyon and High-land Road, Pippa Nolan and Sir Barnaby, Susanna Macaire and Master Marius.

As host nation, Britain was able to enter six individual riders as well as the team, and they went on to win all the medals. The whole squad is seen above with chef d'equipe Lord Patrick Beresford. *Left to right, standing*: Leslie Law, Sarah Cotton, Susanna Macaire, Miles Russell, Anne-Marie Evans, Jane Thelwall. *Sitting*: Polly Lyon, Rodney Powell, Karen Straker, Virginia Leng, Ian Stark and Lorna Clarke. *Left*: Jane Thelwall, and King's Jester, who were competing as individuals, survived a very dramatic 'Look, no hands' moment at the Trout Hatchery to win the silver medal.

Above: Ginny Leng and Master Craftsman, making it look so easy. They led from start to finish, bringing Ginny her third successive European gold medal, which was presented (*above, right*) by the Princess of Wales.
Centre: The gold medal team on their lap of honour: Rodney Powell and The Irishman, Ginny Leng and Priceless, Ian Stark and Glenburnie and Lorna Clarke and Fearliath Mor.
Right: Lorna Clarke and Fearliath Mor, who finished on their dressage score to take the bronze.

At Rotherfield, Polly Lyon achieved a record among the Juniors and Young Riders by winning her third European gold medal - this time on Folly's Last (*left*). Also for a third time she contributed to a team gold. The three other British riders were Lynne Bevan on Horton Point, Daniel Hughes on Fineas Finn and William Fox-Pitt on Steadfast; they led throughout the competition to win a decisive victory over the Germans by more than 140 points.

Above: Lynne Bevan won the silver medal with Horton Point, the horse produced by her sister Ros. In 1994 Lynne had to withdraw from Badminton at the last minute because of injury, and loaned Horton Point to Mark Todd, who rode him to a famous victory. *Right*: The bronze medal winners, Jane Little and Decree Absolute, who were competing as individuals.

The Princess of Wales with Princes William and Harry at the Badminton prizegiving, when the Whitbread Trophy was awarded for the last time after thirty years of sponsorship.

For the third time running in the European Championships, Britain made a clean sweep of the medals. *Above*: Line-up of team, Ian Stark, Mary Thomson, Richard Walker, Karen Straker; and individuals, Lorna Clarke (who had to withdraw King's Jester, lame, after the dressage) and Katie Meacham (who came in 15th on Montana Blue).

Left: The individual gold medal winners Ian Stark and the Maitland-Carews' Glenburnie tackling a fence on Tommy Brennan's beautifully designed and constructed cross-country course.

Above: Richard Walker and Jacana, who won the silver medal, at the first water, where Richard's experience and strong riding prevented a refusal.

Right: Bronze medallists Karen Straker and Get Smart, who had competed together since Pony Club days, in characteristic style on the steeplechase.

For Mary Thomson at her first team appearance it was a less salutary experience. She fell when King William made a huge jump into the water near the finish, and was unable to ride the next day.

A record 12th European team victory for Britain's Juniors brought Rotherfield Park's years as a three-day event venue to a close. Suzanne Donnelly won individual gold for Ireland and Elodie Bernard silver for France, while Britain's Stefanie Thompson *(left)* on Ballyjim II, snatched the bronze by one-fifth of a mark from Heidi Antikatzidis (Greece) *Below:* The British team: Beanie Hughes, Charlotte Wybrew, Michele Parker and Stefanie Thompson.

Horse Trials were initiated at Petworth House in Sussex by local farmer Richard Chandler (*below*) and his wife Flo, who is a keen horsewoman, thus giving event-goers the chance to enjoy this area of outstanding natural beauty

The first project was a cross-country schooling course, designed by Anthony Ffooks (now the event's joint-organiser) and built by him and Richard Chandler (*above*). The Chandlers also run hunter trials and Pony Club one-day events throughout the year, to fit in with the farming calendar.

171

Francis Whittington on Northdown Nova finished with only his dressage penalties to become Britain's first European Pony individual champion. Francis, with Georgie Barnes (Matador), Barney Lee (Brave Buzzard) and Emily Mackenzie (Cottage Gold) won team silver by two-fifths of a mark from Sweden.

Hopetoun House, home of the Marquess of Linlithgow, lies in a majestic setting high above the Firth of Forth. The summer event, which runs over two days, is held to raise money for Multiple Sclerosis. There is an annual event ball, also in aid of MS and to help pay for the cross-country course.

Top: The Forth Road Bridge forms a spectacular back-cloth to the dressage arena. *Centre:* The showground area, where the official tents are supplied by former competitor Mugs Montgomerie. *Left:* Prizes are presented by Rosemary Rollinson of Stirlingshire Saddlery, the event's sponsors, with the Countess of Hopetoun (second from left) and organisers Peter and Grania Dale.

British won the team championship despite the sad loss of James Frederick, ridden by Sarah Cutteridge. The horse had to be put down after cannoning into a tree when jumping into the orchard. *Left*: the individual gold medal winners, Terry Boon and Vital Decision. *Above:* Sarah, on foot, with chef d' équipe Giles Rowsell, trainer Gill Watson, vet Bob Baskerville and other team members Louise Rutherford and The Optimist (silver medallists), Terry Boon, and Daisy Dick and Little Victor.

Britain's all-female team of Mary Thomson, Karen Straker, Charlotte Bathe and Kristina Gifford carried off the gold medal and Karen (*centre left*) on Get Smart won the individual bronze. *Top:* the team and two individuals, Helen Ogden and Caroline Sizer, pose with puppies belonging to Dick Saunders, who stabled their horses for the final trial at Althorp. *Left:* Judy Bradwell, an outstanding rider and producer of horses, was the first FEI lady judge at a World Championships.

Blenheim's first international team championship was for the European Young Riders, with Britain defending both team and individual titles which had been won the year before at Bonn-Rodderberg.

The team (*above*) of Nicola Browne, on Ballyhaise, Polly Clark (Poggio), Terry Boon (Vital Decision) and Emily Thompson (Party Man) scored a comfortable victory over Sweden – despite the well-placed Ballyhaise's failing the final veterinary inspection – with Ireland taking the team bronze medal.

Defending champion Terry Boon led after the cross-country, but a single show jump down let Germany's Gina Melkonian in to take the gold, with Terry (*left*) less than two points behind for the silver.

The British team of Charlotte Bathe on The Cool Customer, Kristina Gifford (Midnight Blue II), William Fox-Pitt (Cosmopolitan II) and Mary King (King William) won both European and Open titles and Mary, seen below performing her dressage test, won the bronze.

Above Tina, Mary, Charlotte and William tucking in to a plate of Pratoni pasta.

Katherine Duckitt brought home from Sweden Britain's only medal, but it was the individual gold, won on her own Joe Brown. The horse was bought from Paddy Muir, out of her home-bred 'Brown 'stable with which she has had so much success.

Blair Castle ran its first international champion-ship, for European Juniors, which attracted entries from eleven nations. The crowds of Scottish supporters were rewarded by the home riders winning team and individual gold medals.

Right: The European Champ-ions, Emma Taylor on her sister Sarah's Fair Dinkum, a son of Welton Apollo and just 15 hands high.

Above: The winning British team with trainer Gill Watson: *left to right*, Emma Taylor, Tom Robinson (who rode California Boy), Stephanie Stark (Go Bust) and Victoria Brewer (Welton Airbourne).

Britain's riders came to the second European Open Championships as defending champions, expecting tough opposition especially from New Zealand and the USA. Since Burghley's official course-designer, Mark Phillips, was also team trainer to the USA, Michael Tucker was appointed to take over the course design.

The British team (*above*) of William Fox-Pitt, riding Cosmopolitan II, Mary King on King William, Ian Stark with Arakai and Christopher Bartle on Word Perfect won the gold medal by 12 points from New Zealand, with Sweden third.

Like the individual Open gold medallist Mark Todd, who rode Broadcast News, William Fox-Pitt (*right*) finished on his dressage score to win the Open bronze and European silver medals.

Right: Kristina Gifford and General Jock retained their dressage score to finish sixth overall but were awarded the European bronze medal because the riders placed above them, Blyth Tait and Vaughn Jefferis, were New-Zealanders.

Below: Team vet Andy Bathe in discussion with Giles Rowsell, International Team Committee Chairman and senior chef d' équipe of the British team for the first time.

Below: The Princess Royal with Philip Herbert, clerk of the course, and Burghley Chairman Dick Saunders, standing on the promontory built out into the lake to provide access to the new obstacles in the water under Lion Bridge.

Bill Lithgow, who died in 1997, was from 1965 until 1976 an inspiring leader of the British team as chef d'équipe. During that period Britain won six team gold medals in succession, two of them Olympic, plus two silver and two bronze, and individual medals, including one Olympic, three World and three European golds. A former CO of the King's Troop RHA and of the 10th Hussars he was for 17 years Executive Director of The Pony Club.

Christopher Bartle had achieved Britain's highest Olympic Dressage placing – sixth at Los Angeles 1984 on Wily Trout – before he returned full-time to eventing and was appointed official dressage trainer to the three-day event team.

In 1997 at Thirlestane he won the Scottish Open Championships on Word Perfect (sold on to Mr and Mrs Adrian Cantwell so that the successful partnership could continue) and was a member of Britain's gold-medal team at Burghley. On that occasion his was the discard score, but at Badminton his flawless performance on Word Perfect brought him a very popular victory.

Britain's Pony Three-Day Event team joined their show jumping and dressage colleagues at Le Touquet in Normandy for the annual European Pony Championships, and came away with the individual gold for Kim Levan, and the team silver.

Pony Championships had already run for some years on the continent, and towards the end of the '80s Tinka Taylor, chairman of the British Pony show jumpers, encouraged the three-day eventers to form a team. Built around successful Pony Club riders and dependent on their own family resources, they always came home with a medal. In 1988, under Mrs Jane Whiteley's chairmanship, they were officially brought into the Horse Trials fold. In 1992 Mrs Laurence Rook took over as chairman, retiring in 1998 after seeing her team winning the medals at Le Touquet.

Above: Kim Levan riding Harry Hotshot on the big and imposing cross-country course. Their clear show jumping round secured the gold medal. *Right*: Team silver medallists (*left to right*) Kitty Boggis, Amy Williams, Catherine Wilson and Kim Levan.

Medals Won by Great Britain
in International Three-Day Events

Olympic Games

1936 - Berlin
Team Bronze
Capt. R. Fanshawe / Bowie Knife
Lt. E. Howard-Vyse / Blue Steel
Capt. A. Scott / Bob Clive

1956 - Stockholm
Team Gold
Lt-Col. Frank Weldon / Kilbarry
Major Laurence Rook / Wild Venture
Bertie Hill / Countryman III
Individual Bronze
Lt.-Col. Frank Weldon / Kilbarry

1968 - Mexico City
Team Gold
Major Derek Allhusen / Lochinvar
Richard Meade / Cornishman V
Sgt. Ben Jones RHA / The Poacher
Jane Bullen / Our Nobby
Individual Silver
Major Derek Allhusen

1972 - Munich
Team Gold
Richard Meade / Laurieston
Mary Gordon Watson / Cornishman V
Bridget Parker / Cornish Gold
Lt. Mark Phillips / Great Ovation
Individual Gold
Richard Meade / Laurieston

1984 - Los Angeles
Team Silver
Virginia Holgate / Priceless
Lucinda Green / Regal Realm
Ian Stark / Oxford Blue
Diana Clapham / Windjammer
Individual Bronze
Virginia Holgate / Priceless

1988 - Seoul
Team Silver
Ian Stark / Sir Wattie
Virginia Leng / Master Craftsman
Karen Straker / Get Smart
Capt. Mark Phillips / Cartier
Individual Silver
Ian Stark / Sir Wattie
Individual Bronze
Virginia Leng / Master Craftsman

World Championships

1966 - Burghley
Individual Silver
Richard Meade / Barberry

1970 - Punchestown
Team Gold
Mary Gordon-Watson / Cornishman V
Richard Meade / The Poacher

Lt. Mark Phillips / Chicago III
Stuart Stevens / Benson
Individual Gold
Mary Gordon Watson / Cornishman V
Individual Silver
Richard Meade / The Poacher

1974 - Burghley
Team Silver
Richard Meade / Wayfarer II
Bridget Parker / Cornish Gold
Christopher Collins / Smokey VI
Capt. Mark Phillips / Columbus
Individual Bronze
Hugh Thomas / Playamar

1982 - Luhmühlen
Team Gold
Lucinda Green / Regal Realm
Richard Meade / Kilcashel
Virginia Holgate / Priceless
Rachel Bayliss / Mystic Minstrel
Individual Gold
Lucinda Green / Regal Realm

1986 - Gawler
Team Gold
Virginia Leng / Priceless
Lorna Clarke / Myross
Ian Stark / Oxford Blue
Clarissa Strachan / Delphy Dazzle
Individual Gold
Virginia Leng / Priceless
Individual Bronze
Lorna Clarke / Myross

1986 - Bialy Bor
C.C.I.O.
Team Gold
Virginia Leng / Night Cap II
Ian Stark / Sir Wattie
Rachel Hunt / Piglet II
Madeleine Gurdon / The Done Thing
Individual Gold
Virginia Leng / Night Cap II
Individual Bronze
Ian Stark / Sir Wattie

1990 - Stockholm
W.E.G.
Team Silver
Ian Stark / Murphy Himself
Rodney Powell / The Irishman II
Karen Straker / Get Smart
Virginia Leng / Griffin
Individual Silver
Ian Stark / Murphy Himself

1994 - The Hague
W.E.G.
Team Gold
Karen Dixon / Get Smart
Mary Thomson / King William
Charlotte Bathe / The Cool Customer
Kristina Gifford / General Jock
Individual Bronze
Karen Dixon / Get Smart

1998 - Pratoni del Vivaro
W.E.G.
Team Bronze
Polly Phillips / Coral Cove
Gary Parsonage / Magic Rogue
Nigel Taylor / The Frenchman
Karen Dixon / Too Smart

European Championships

1953 - Badminton
Team Gold
Major Frank Weldon / Kilbarry
Reg Hindley / Speculation
Bertie Hill / Bambi V
Individual Gold
Major Laurence Rook / Starlight XV
Individual Silver
Major Frank Weldon / Kilbarry

1954 - Basle
Team Gold
Bertie Hill / Crispin
Major Frank Weldon / Kilbarry
Major Laurence Rook / Starlight XV
Diana Mason / Tramella
Individual Gold
Bertie Hill / Crispin
Individual Silver
Major Frank Weldon / Kilbarry
Individual Bronze
Major Laurence Rook / Starlight XV

1955 - Windsor
Team Gold
Major Frank Weldon / Kilbarry
Bertie Hill / Countryman III
Major Laurence Rook / Starlight XV
Diana Mason / Tramella
Individual Gold
Major Frank Weldon / Kilbarry
Individual Silver
Lt. Cmdr John Oram / Radar
Individual Bronze
Bertie Hill / Countryman III

1957 - Copenhagen
Team Gold
Sheila Willcox / High and Mighty
Ted Marsh / Wild Venture
Major Derek Allhusen / Laurien
Kit Tatham-Warter / Pampas Cat
Individual Gold
Sheila Willcox / High and Mighty

1959 - Harewood
Team Silver
Lt. Col. Frank Weldon / Samuel Johnson
Major Derek Allhusen / Laurien
Jeremy Beale / Fulmer Folly
Sheila Waddington / Airs and Graces
Individual Silver
Lt. Col. Frank Weldon / Samuel Johnson
Individual Bronze
Major Derek Allhusen / Laurien

185

1962 - Burghley
Individual Gold
Capt. James Templer / M'Lord Connolly
Individual Bronze
Jane Wykeham-Musgrave / Ryebrooks*Team Bronze*
Lt-Col. Frank Weldon / Young Pretender
Michael Bullen / Sea Breeze
Susan Fleet / The Gladiator
Capt. Peter Welch / Mister Wilson

1965 - Moscow
Team Bronze
Major Derek Allhusen / Lochinvar
Richard Meade / Barberry
Christine Sheppard / Fenjirao
Sgt. Ben Jones / Master Bernard

1967 - Punchestown
Team Gold
Capt. Martin Whiteley / The Poacher
Major Derek Allhusen / Lochinvar
Sgt. Ben Jones / Foxdor
Richard Meade / Barberry
Individual Silver
Capt. Martin Whiteley / The Poacher
Individual Bronze
Major Derek Allhusen / Lochinvar

1969 - Haras du Pin
Team Gold
Richard Walker / Pasha
Major Derek Allhusen / Lochinvar
Pollyann Hely-Hutchinson / Count Jasper
S/Sgt Ben Jones / The Poacher
Individual Gold
Mary Gordon Watson / Cornishman V
Individual Silver
Richard Walker / Pasha

1971 - Burghley
Team Gold
Debbie West / Baccarat
Mary Gordon Watson / Cornishman V
Richard Meade / The Poacher
Lt. Mark Phillips / Great Ovation
Individual Gold
H.R.H. The Princess Anne / Doublet
Individual Silver
Debbie West / Baccarat
Individual Bronze
Stuart Stevens / Classic Chips

1973 - Kiev
Team Bronze
Richard Meade / Wayfarer II
Lucinda Prior-Palmer / Be Fair
Janet Hodgson / Larkspur
Debbie West / Baccarat

1975 - Luhmühlen
Individual Gold
Lucinda Prior-Palmer / Be Fair
Individual Silver
H.R.H The Princess Anne / Goodwill
Team Silver
Lucinda Prior-Palmer / Be Fair
H.R.H The Princess Anne / Goodwill
Sue Hatherly / Harley
Janet Hodgson / Larkspur

1977 - Burghley
Team Gold
Lucinda Prior-Palmer / George

Jane Holderness-Roddam / Warrior
Christopher Collins / Smokey VI
Clarissa Strachan / Merry Sovereign
Individual Gold
Lucinda Prior-Palmer / George

1979 - Luhmühlen
Team Silver
Sue Hatherly / Monacle II
Christopher Collins / Gamble
Clarissa Strachan / Merry Sovereign
Lucinda Prior-Palmer / Killaire
Individual Silver
Rachel Bayliss / Gurgle The Greek

1981 - Horsens
Team Gold
Virginia Holgate / Priceless
Richard Meade / Kilcashel
Sue Benson / Gemma Jay
Elizabeth Purbrick / Peter The Great

1983 - Frauenfeld
Individual Gold
Rachel Bayliss / Mystic Minstrel
Individual Silver
Lucinda Green / Regal Realm
Team Silver
Lucinda Green / Regal Realm
Virginia Holgate / Night Cap II
Lorna Clarke / Danville
Diana Clapham / Windjammer II

1985 - Burghley
Team Gold
Virginia Leng / Priceless
Lorna Clarke / Myross
Ian Stark / Oxford Blue
Lucinda Green / Regal Realm
Individual Gold
Virginia Leng / Priceless
Individual Silver
Lorna Clarke / Myross

1987 - Luhmühlen
Team Gold
Virginia Leng / Night Cap II
Ian Stark / Sir Wattie
Rachel Hunt / Aloaf
Lucinda Green / Shannagh
Individual Gold
Virginia Leng / Night Cap II
Individual Silver
Ian Stark / Sir Wattie

1989 - Burghley
Team Gold
Virginia Leng / Master Craftsman
Lorna Clarke / Fearliath Mor
Ian Stark / Glenburnie
Rodney Powell / The Irishman II
Individual Gold
Virginia Leng / Master Craftsman
Individual Silver
Jane Thelwall / King's Jester
Individual Bronze
Lorna Clarke / Fearliath Mor

1991 - Punchestown
Team Gold
Ian Stark / Glenburnie
Richard Walker / Jacana
Karen Straker / Get Smart
Mary Thomson / King William

Individual Gold
Ian Stark / Glenburnie
Individual Silver
Richard Walker / Jacana
Individual Bronze
Karen Straker / Get Smart

1993 - Achselschwang
Individual Silver
Kristina Gifford / Song and Dance Man

1995 - Pratoni del Vivaro
Team Gold
Mary King / King William
William Fox-Pitt / Cosmopolitan II
Kristina Gifford / Midnight Blue II
Charlotte Bathe / The Cool Customer
Individual Bronze
Mary King / King William

1995 - Pratoni del Vivaro OPEN
Team Gold
Mary King / King William
William Fox-Pitt / Cosmopolitian II
Kristina Gifford / Midnight Blue II
Charlotte Bathe / The Cool Customer
Individual Bronze
Mary King / King William

1997 - Burghley
Team Gold
William Fox-Pitt / Cosmopolitan II
Mary King / Star Appeal
Ian Stark / Arakai
Christopher Bartle / Word Perfect II
Individual Silver
William Fox-Pitt / Cosmopolitan II
Individual Bronze
Kristina Gifford / General Jock

1997 - Burghley OPEN
Team Gold
William Fox-Pitt / Cosmopolitan II
Mary King / Star Appeal
Ian Stark / Arakai
Christopher Bartle / Word Perfect II
Individual Bronze
William Fox-Pitt / Cosmopolitain II

European Junior Championships

1967 - Eridge
No Team Competition
Individual Silver
Richard Walker

1968 - Craon
Individual Gold
Richard Walker / Pasha
Team Silver
Richard Walker / Pasha
Angela Sowden / Clorinda
Stuart Stevens / Benson
Tessa Borwick / Sermonetto

1969 - Euskirchen
Individual Bronze
Aly Pattinson / Sharon

1970 - Holsterbo
Team Bronze
   Christopher Brooke / Olive Oyl
   Mary Warren / Yogi Bear
   Peter Raymond / Tawstock Gent
   Tony Hill / Chicago III

1971 - Wesel
Team Gold
   Christopher Brooke / Olive Oyl
   Amanda Sivewright / Gameel
   Lucinda Prior-Palmer / Be Fair
   Andrew Brake / Say When
Individual Gold
   Christopher Brooke / Olive Oyl

1972 - Eridge
Team Gold
   Tony Hill / Maid Marion
   Amanda Sivewright / Alsedell
   Alex Colquhoun / Belle Grey
   Christopher Brooke / Olive Oyl
Individual Silver
   Tony Hill / Maid Marion

1973 - Pompadour
Team Gold
   Virginia Holgate / Dubonnet
   Sara Bailey / Red Amber
   Annabel Scrimgeour / Lysander II
   Dawn Brands / Just A Cloud
Individual Gold
   Virginia Holgate / Dubonnet
Individual Silver
   Sara Bailey / Red Amber

1974 - Pratoni del Vivaro
Individual Gold
   Sheila Ker / Peer Gynt
Individual Bronze
   Joanna Winter / Stainless Steel

1976 - Lage - Siekkrug
Team Gold
   Debbie Saffell / Double Brandy
   Sarah Bouet / Sea Lord V
   Fraser Jack / Burnt Oak
   Caroline Saunders / Cymbal
Individual Silver
   Debbie Saffell / Double Brandy
Individual Bronze
   Sarah Bouet / Sea Lord V

1979 - Punchestown
Individual Gold
   Nicola May / Commodore IV
Team Silver
   Nicola May / Commodore IV
   Sarah Calloway / Bassanio
   'Tuffy' Tilley / Tom Temp
   Brigit Ensten / Carbrooke Charles

1980 - Achselschwang
Team Gold
   Claire Needham / Solo
   Susanna Brooke / Super Star IV
   Nicola May / Commodore IV
   Virginia Strawson / Greek Herb
Individual Silver
   Claire Needham / Solo

1981 - Saint Fargeau
Team Silver
   Virginia Strawson / Greek Herb

   Timothy Dudgeon / Tom Faggus
   Polly Schwerdt / Dylan II
   Georgina Sandell / Moss II

1982 - Rotherfield Park
Team Gold
   Karen Straker / Running Bear
   Anne-Marie Taylor / Gin and Orange
   Katherine Gracey / Rustic Rambler
   Ros Bevan / Horton Venture
Individual Gold
   Karen Straker / Running Bear

1983 - Pratoni del Vivaro
Team Gold
   Helen Brown / Fleetwood Opposition
   Sarah Williams / Spiritos
   Susanna Macaire / Latin Tempo
   Rachel Hunt / Friday Fox
Individual Gold
   Helen Brown / Fleetwood Opposition

1984 - Drzonkow
Team Silver
   Melanie Gurdon / The Done Thing
   Jonathan Gooderham / Rustic Moon
   Jamie Search / Capricorn VI
   Katie Parker / Master Chester
Individual Silver
   Melanie Gurdon / The Done Thing

1985 - Rotherfield Park
Team Gold
   Alexandra Ramus / Spy Story II
   Clea Hoeg / Norton Boy
   Sally Bateson / Scalphunter
   Steven Chambers / Talisman SC
Individual Bronze
   Georgina Anstee / Printer's Devil

1986 - Walldorf
Individual Silver
   Polly Martin / Krugerrand
Team Bronze
   Polly Martin / Krugerrand
   Susan Cope / Juicy Lucy
   Pippa Nolan / Airborne III
   Simon Hazlem / Gang Star

1987 - Pratoni del Vivaro
Team Gold
   Polly Lyon / Highland Road
   Claire Bowley / Fair Share
   Andrea Morris / Jack O'Lantern
   Kristina Gifford / Song and Dance Man
Individual Gold
   Polly Lyon / Highland Road
Individual Silver
   William Fox-Pitt / Steadfast

1988 - Dijon - Bonvaux
Team Gold
   Kristina Gifford / Smithstown Lad
   Alice Clapham / Bowmanhill Crystal Clear
   Sophie Newman / Blackmore Money Spinner
   David England / Chevy Chase
Individual Bronze
   Kristina Gifford / Smithstown Lad

1990 - Vittel
Team Silver
   Sarah Cutteridge / Harry's Boy
   Elisabeth Bulmer / Wilsummer Master M
   Rosie Gunn / Croft Maghera
   Stefanie Thompson / Ballyjim II

1991 - Rotherfield Park
Team Gold
   Stefanie Thompson / Ballyjim II
   Davina Hughes / Jenny Black
   Charlotte Wybrew / Withcote Freddie
   Michelle Parker / Crot
Individual Bronze
   Stefanie Thompson / Ballyjim II

1993 - Loughanmore
Team Silver
   Lucy Wiegersma / Custard
   Panda Wilson / Freddie Mercury
   Nigel Lynn / Ruckley's Best
   Sarah England / Goosey Lucy
Individual Silver
   Lucy Wiegersma / Custard

1994 - Pratoni del Vivaro
Team Bronze
   Kirsty Hynd / Work of Art
   Ali Wilkes / Lord Polo
   Lucy Wiegersma / Woodstown Boy
   Panda Wilson / Court Command
Individual Bronze
   Kirsty Hynd / Work of Art

1995 - Bunge - Gotland
Individual Gold
   Katherine Duckitt / Joe Brown

1996 - Blair Castle
Team Gold
   Emma Taylor / Fair Dinkum
   Tom Robinson / Califonia Boy
   Victoria Brewer / Welton Airbourne
   Stephanie Stark / Go Bust
Individual Gold
   Emma Taylor / Fair Dinkum

1998 - Bialy Bor
Team Gold
   Emilie Chandler / Weston Mikris
   Sophy Ames / Dance
   Emily Baldwin / Welton Airbourne
   Jenny Julian / Rathmore Diamond
Individual Silver
   Emilie Chandler / Weston Mikris

European Young Rider Championships

1981 - Achselschwang
Team Gold
   Lucy Bywater / The Countryman
   Maureen Piggott / Asian Princess
   Beverley Thomas / Divine Intervention
   Sheena Trevett / Unusual

1982 - Fontainebleau
Individual Gold
   Virginia Strawson / Minsmore
Team Silver
   Virginia Strawson / Minsmore
   Sarah Callaway / Bassanio
   Maureen Piggott / Hong Kong Discoverer
   Frances Hunter / Strike-a-Light

1983 - Burghley
Team Gold
　　Karen Straker / Running Bear
　　Polly Schwerdt / Dylan II
　　Virginia Strawson / Minsmore
　　Camilla Murdoch / Rugan
Individual Silver
　　Karen Straker / Running Bear
Individual Bronze
　　Polly Schwerdt / Dylan II

1984 - Luhmühlen
Team Gold
　　Rachel Hunt / Friday Fox
　　Jonquil Sainsbury / Hassan
　　Polly Schwerdt / Dylan II
　　Mandy Orchard / Coeur de Lion
Individual Silver
　　Philippa Magill / Headley Bravo
Individual Bronze
　　Rachel Hunt / Friday Fox

1985 - Le Lion d'Angers
Team Gold
　　Claire Oseman / Another Fred
　　Rachel Hunt / Friday Fox
　　Anne-Marie Taylor / Justyn Thyme VI
　　Ros Bevan / Horton Venture
Individual Gold
　　Claire Oseman / Another Fred

1986 - Rotherfield Park
Team Gold
　　Vanessa Ashbourne / Hector James
　　Rachel Hunt / Friday Fox
　　Julie-Anne Shield / Crimdon Lucky George
　　Judith Copland / Sweeney
Individual Gold
　　Alexandra Ramus / Spy Story II
Individual Silver
　　Vanessa Ashbourne / Hector James
Individual Bronze
　　Rachel Hunt / Friday Fox

1987 - Bialy Bor
Individual Gold
　　Pippa Nolan / Sir Barnaby

1988 - Limburg-Zonhoven
Team Gold
　　Polly Lyon / Highland Road
　　William Fox-Pitt / Steadfast
　　Pippa Nolan / Sir Barnaby
　　Susanna Macaire / Master Marius
Individual Gold
　　Polly Lyon / Highland Road

1989 - Achselschwang
Team Silver
　　Pippa Nolan / Sir Barnaby
　　William Fox-Pitt / Steadfast
　　Kristina Gifford / Smithstown Lad
　　Daniel Hughes / Finneas Finn
Individual Silver
　　Pippa Nolan / Sir Barnaby
Individual Bronze
　　William Fox-Pitt / Steadfast

1990 - Rotherfield Park
Team Gold
　　Polly Lyon / Folly's Last
　　Lynne Bevan / Horton Point
　　William Fox-Pitt / Steadfast
　　Daniel Hughes / Finneas Finn
Individual Gold
　　Polly Lyon / Folly's Last
Individual Silver
　　Lynne Bevan / Horton Point
Individual Bronze
　　Jane Little / Decree Absolute

1991 - Turin
Team Bronze
　　Lynne Bevan / Horton Point
　　Kristina Gifford / Smithstown Lad
　　Cara Ball / T.R. Miniking
　　Lucy Jennings / Diamond Pedlar
Individual Bronze
　　Lynne Bevan / Decree Absolute II

1992 - Compiègne
Team Bronze
　　Emma-Jane Jones / Greenside Oliver
　　Sophie Newman / Chris Starskey
　　Lucy Jennings / Diamond Pedlar
　　Daisy Dick / Headley Bravo
Individual Bronze
　　Emma-Jane Jones / Greenside Oliver

1993 - Bonn-Rodderberg
Team Gold
　　Terry Boon / Vital Decision
　　Louise Rutherford / The Optimist
　　Daisy Dick / Little Victor
　　Sarah Cutteridge / James Frederick
Individual Gold
　　Terry Boon / Vital Decision
Individual Silver
　　Louise Rutherford / The Optimist

1994 - Blenheim
Team Gold
　　Terry Boon / Vital Decision
　　Polly Clark / Poggio
　　Emily Thompson / Party Man
　　Nicola Browne / Ballyhaise
Individual Silver
　　Terry Boon / Vital Decision

1995 - Achselschwang
Team Silver
　　Laura Jennings / Time Watch
　　Jamie Atkinson / Salerosa
　　Julie Tew / Henry Tudor IV
　　Nicola Browne / Ballyhaise

1997 - Pratoni del Vivaro
Team Bronze
　　Sacha Pemble / Kiltinane Spot
　　Camilla Hall / Just So II
　　Annabel Collins / Dear Sir
　　Julie Robinson / Irish Skater

European Pony Championships

1987 - Saumur
Team Bronze
　　Cilla Backhouse/Squirrel Nutkin
　　Charlotte Wybrew/Ampersand
　　David England/Master Tilton
　　Amelia Beeston/Just Gambit

1988 - Knuthenborg
Individual Silver
Nicola Browne/Gunnerby Quality Street

1989 - Millstreet
Team Silver
　　Nicola Browne/Gunnerby Quality Street
　　Camilla Whitely/Thistledown Grove
　　Julie Tew/Hailes Emir
　　Sarah Ann Gunn/The Minstrel
Individual Silver
　　Nicola Browne/Gunnerby Quality Street

1990 - Pratoni del Vivaro
Team Bronze
　　Nicola Browne/Gunnerby Quality Street
　　Sarah Ann Gunn/The Minstrel
　　Becky Canham/Matador
　　Kathryn Ellis/Flying Song
Individual Bronze
　　Nicola Browne/Gunnerby Quality Street

1991 - Wierden/Diepenheim
Team Gold
　　Sara England/Confey Star
　　Holly Griffiths/Yeolands Silver Blade
　　Becky Canham/Hewood Silver Flute
　　Joe Turner/Criffel Capulet
Indivudal Bronze
　　Holly Griffths/Yeolands Silver Blade

1993 - Hasselt
Team Silver
　　Francis Whittington/Northdown Nova
　　Georgie Barnes/Matador
　　Emily Mackenzie/Cottage Gold
　　Barney Lee/Brave Buzzard
Individual Gold
　　Francis Whittington/Northdown Nova

1995 - Achselschwang
Team Silver
　　Charlotte Le Sueur/Treworval Herbi
　　Victoria Brewer/Yogi Bear
　　Jessica Waley-Cohen/ The Minstrel
　　Alexi Mackinnon/Britvic
Individual Silver
　　Charlotte Le Sueur/Treworval Herbi

1996 - Barthahus
Team Bronze
　　Helen Bosanquet/Sapphire Blue
　　Charlotte Le Sueur/Treworval Herbi
　　Bryony Whittington/Northdown Nova
　　Lyndsay McDonald/Will-O-The-Wisp

1998 - Le Touquet
Team Silver
　　Kim Levan/Harry Hotshot
　　Kitty Boggis/Red Alert
　　Catherine Wilson/Mulacash Tammy
　　Amy Williams/Donadea Sandmarshall
Individual Gold
　　Kim Levan/Harry Hotshot

Index

Acknowledgments & Credits

Acknowledgments

The Editor and Publishers acknowledge with many thanks the help given by the following:
Mr and Mrs Sam Barr, Mrs Henry Batten, Mrs Clarissa Bleakman, Mrs Diana Bown, Rosemary Lady Brookeborough, Mrs Sally Bullen, Mr Duncan Burns, Mrs Christopher Bywater, Mrs Richard Chandler, Mrs Lorna Clarke, Miss Emma Collings, Mr Alex Colquhoun, Mrs Rachel Commander, Mrs Brian Crago, Lady Courtenay, Colonel del Force, Mrs Srdja Djukanovic, Mrs N Elgar, Mr D Engleheart, Mr W Fox-Pitt, The Honourable Heather Galbraith, Mr David Gardiner, Miss Nici Gibb, Mrs Althea Gifford, Mr Jim Gilmore, Miss Mary Gordon Watson, Mrs Tom Greenhalgh, Mrs Dick Hawkins, Mrs Bill Henson, Mrs Bertie Hill, Colonel Peter Hodgson, Mrs Heather Holgate, Horse and Hound, Hothouse Media, Miss Elizabeth Inman, Elisabeth Lady Joicey, Mrs Bridget Joynson, The Honourable Mrs (Ghislaine) Kennerley, Mrs Mary King, The Honourable Mrs (Daphne) Lakin, Mrs Marjorie Langford, Mrs Michael Lanz, Mrs Cynthia Llewellen-Palmer, Mrs Audrey Ann Lockett, Mrs Elisabeth Macfarlane, Mrs Peggy Maxwell, Mrs Janet McFarling, Mrs Jenny McGregor, Miss Alex Medhurst, Mrs Debbie Melville, Colonel John Mennell, Miss Sally Merrick, Midland Bank, Mrs Larry Moore, Mrs Chris Morgan-Owen, Mrs Sarah Munnings, Mrs George Nolan, Mr Michael Poland, Mr Michael Rudge, Mr Christopher Schofield, Mrs Robin Scrimgeour, Mr Michael Skinner, Mrs Veronica Spackman, Mrs Toby Sturgis, Brigadier James Templer, Miss Eileen Thomas, Mrs Elizabeth Walker, Miss Gill Watson, Mrs Frank Weldon, Miss Sheila Willcox, Mrs John Waterhouse, Mrs Barry Wookey, Miss Jane Wykeham-Musgrave.
The medal tables on pages 185 to 188 were complied by Rhydain Wynn-Williams.

Picture Credits

Abbreviations: t = top, b = bottom, l = left, r = right, c = centre.

Kit Houghton: Cover photograph and pages 110 (bl), 113, 122 (t), 129, 130 (cl,cr), 133 (c,br), 134 (tl), 135, 136 (c, bl), 137, 138 (t), 139 (b), 143, 144 (t), 145 (t), 146 (bl), 147 (t,cr,bl), 150 (t), 152 (t), 153 (t,b), 158, 159, 160, 161, 164, 165, 166, 168 (b), 169, 170, 171, 174, 175 (cl,r,b), 176,177, 180, 184. *Horse & Hound Library:* 20 (t,cr,br), 21 (cr,br), 25 (sketchmap), 26 (t), 29 (c), 30 (t,b, 39, 41 (b), 42, 47, 58, 59, 67, 76 (b), 81 (t), 82 (b,l,r), 93, 100 (Trevor Meeks, br), 101 (Trevor Meeks, br), 118 (c,bl), 180/1/3 (Trevor Meeks). *Leslie Lane*: 22 (b), 45, 61 (c), 64 (b), 86 (b), 90 (b), 95 (b), 121 (b), 130 (t). *Cyril Diamond*: 54 (c,b), 62 (t, br), 65, 69 (t), 107 (tl,bl), 119. *Midland Bank* : 36 (t), 37 (b) 66 (b), 67 (t), 77, 78, 82 (t), 83, 84, 87 (b), 94, 102 (bl &r). *Srdja Djukanovic:* Frontspiece, back cover and pages 90 (t), 103 (t), 142, 167, 168, 175, 180. *Findlay Davidson*: 68, 72, 84 (b), 85 (t), 91 (b), 99 (b), 102 (t), 105, 109, 112, 136 (br), 144 (b). *Jim Meads*: 128, 133 (t), 136 (cl), 145 (b); Jean Bridel 23,33 (b); Peter Pritchard 24 (t); Foto Tiedmann 25 (t); Monty 27; Col. J.Mennell 29 (t,b), Western Morning News 32 (b); Rex Coleman 35; D.M.Smith 36 (b); Chatsworth House 38 (t); Planet News 40 (c); Svenskt Pressfoto 40 (b); Associated Press 41 (t), Expo Life 49 (t); P.A.Reuter 50; Press Association 138 (bl); Sydney Morning Herald 51 (t); Miles Bros 51 (b); Bill Robinson 53 (bl); Envoy Press Photos 54 (b); Lotta Ostman 57 (b); Clive Hiles 61 (t), 76 (t), 88 (t); Frank H. Meads   62 (bl), David Robinson 63; Studio Guillox 71 (t); Charles C. Fennel 89; Times Newspapers 91 (t); Foto Mitschko 92 (t); John Corsan 110 (t); Stuart Newsham 118 (tr,bl), 134 (tr,c,b),140,146 (t,br), 147 (cl,br); Jennie Walton 120 (t); Barn Owl 121 (c); Horseman Photography 123 (t,b); Sue Allfrey 123 (c); Spicer Hallfield 124 (b); Hugo M.Czerny 126; Peter Hogan 120 (b); Desmond O'Neill 136 (tl); Nick Morris 17.
The watercolours are by Tim Taylor, and the pencil drawings on pages 14,15 and 16 are from the BHTA archives.
Note: Illustrations not listed above are those which have been loaned privately and/or for which the photographers are not known. In some cases it has not been possible to trace copyright holders, and we apologise for these omissions and would welcome any relevant information.

STOP PRESS

Britain won the 1988 European Junior Championships at Bialy Bor, in Poland,when the team of Emilie Chandler (individual silver medal), Emily Baldwin, Sophy Ames and Jenny Julian beat the host nation in a close finish. At the World Equestrian Games at Pratoni, in Italy, the British team, having already lost several of its most experienced horses and riders, went consistently well – putting up the best cross-country performance out of all the nations – to win the bronze medal behind New Zealand and France. The team consisted of Polly Phillipps, Gary Parsonage, Nigel Taylor and Karen Dixon, with individuals Peta Beckett and Jeanette Brakewell.